THE BEDFORD SERIES IN HISTORY AND CULTURE

Religious Transformations in the Early Modern World

A Brief History with Documents

Related Titles in
THE BEDFORD SERIES IN HISTORY AND CULTURE
Advisory Editors: Lynn Hunt, *University of California, Los Angeles*
David W. Blight, *Yale University*
Bonnie G. Smith, *Rutgers University*
Natalie Zemon Davis, *Princeton University*
Ernest R. May, *Harvard University*

Power and the Holy in the Age of the Investiture Conflict: A Brief History with Documents
   Maureen C. Miller, *University of California, Berkeley*

Christopher Columbus and the Enterprise of the Indies: A Brief History with Documents
   Geoffrey Symcox, *University of California, Los Angeles*, and Blair Sullivan, *University of California, Los Angeles*

Victors and Vanquished: Spanish and Nahua Views of the Conquest of Mexico
   Edited with an Introduction by Stuart B. Schwartz, *Yale University*

UTOPIA *by Sir Thomas More*
   Edited with an Introduction by David Harris Sacks, *Reed College*

The Saint Bartholomew's Day Massacre: A Brief History with Documents
   Barbara B. Diefendorf, *Boston University*

THE DISCOVERY OF GUIANA *by Sir Walter Ralegh with Related Documents*
   Edited with an Introduction by Benjamin Schmidt, *University of Washington*

THE JESUIT RELATIONS: *Natives and Missionaries in Seventeenth-Century North America*
   Edited with an Introduction by Allan Greer, *University of Toronto*

THE BEDFORD SERIES IN HISTORY AND CULTURE

Religious Transformations in the Early Modern World

A Brief History with Documents

Merry E. Wiesner-Hanks

University of Wisconsin–Milwaukee

BEDFORD/ST. MARTIN'S   Boston ◆ New York

For Bedford/St. Martin's

Publisher for History: Mary V. Dougherty
Director of Development for History: Jane Knetzger
Senior Editor: Heidi L. Hood
Senior Developmental Editor: Louise Townsend
Editorial Assistants: Katherine Flynn, Jennifer Jovan
Production Associate: Samuel Jones
Executive Marketing Manager: Jenna Bookin Barry
Text Design: Claire Seng-Niemoeller
Project Management: Books By Design, Inc.
Index: Books By Design, Inc.
Cover Design: Joy Lin
Cover Art: *Emperor Akbar and the Jesuits*, from *The History of Akbar* (Akbarnama), painted by Nor Singh, ca. 1605, India. © The Trustees of the Chester Beatty Library, Dublin.
Composition: TexTech International
Printing and Binding: RR Donnelley & Sons Company

President: Joan E. Feinberg
Editorial Director: Denise B. Wydra
Director of Marketing: Karen R. Soeltz
Director of Editing, Design, and Production: Marcia Cohen
Assistant Director of Editing, Design, and Production: Elise S. Kaiser
Manager, Publishing Services: Emily Berleth

Library of Congress Control Number: 2008933816

Manufactured in the United States of America.

3 2 1 0 9 8
f e d c b a

For information, write: Bedford/St. Martin's, 75 Arlington Street, Boston, MA 02116   (617-399-4000)

ISBN-10: 0-312-45886-X
ISBN-13: 978-0-312-45886-7

Acknowledgments

Acknowledgments and copyrights appear at the back of the book on pages 172–73, which constitute an extension of the copyright page.

Foreword

The Bedford Series in History and Culture is designed so that readers can study the past as historians do.

The historian's first task is finding the evidence. Documents, letters, memoirs, interviews, pictures, movies, novels, or poems can provide facts and clues. Then the historian questions and compares the sources. There is more to do than in a courtroom, for hearsay evidence is welcome, and the historian is usually looking for answers beyond act and motive. Different views of an event may be as important as a single verdict. How a story is told may yield as much information as what it says.

Along the way the historian seeks help from other historians and perhaps from specialists in other disciplines. Finally, it is time to write, to decide on an interpretation and how to arrange the evidence for readers.

Each book in this series contains an important historical document or group of documents, each document a witness from the past and open to interpretation in different ways. The documents are combined with some element of historical narrative—an introduction or a biographical essay, for example—that provides students with an analysis of the primary source material and important background information about the world in which it was produced.

Each book in the series focuses on a specific topic within a specific historical period. Each provides a basis for lively thought and discussion about several aspects of the topic and the historian's role. Each is short enough (and inexpensive enough) to be a reasonable one-week assignment in a college course. Whether as classroom or personal reading, each book in the series provides firsthand experience of the challenge— and fun—of discovering, recreating, and interpreting the past.

Lynn Hunt
David W. Blight
Bonnie G. Smith
Natalie Zemon Davis
Ernest R. May

Preface

The cover of this book depicts scholars from many religious traditions, including Muslims, Hindus, Zoroastrians, Sikhs, and Christians, gathered together at the court of the Mughal emperor Akbar in the 1580s. Akbar was fascinated by religion, and the discussions and debates at his court were often contentious, with the emperor playing an active part in them, challenging and questioning. Not satisfied with simply debating the merits of existing religions, in 1582 Akbar created a new religion that blended ideas and ceremonies from several traditions into what he termed the "Divine Faith."

The debates at Akbar's court and his creation of the Divine Faith are examples of religious transformations that occurred in many parts of the world in the fifteenth and sixteenth centuries: global interactions among adherents of different religious traditions and innovations that altered existing religions dramatically or created entirely new faiths. Yet the scene at Akbar's court was also atypical, for interactions among people of different religious traditions more often involved force and bloodshed than peaceful discussion. This had been true throughout world history, of course, but the global scope of religious interactions in this era was unprecedented.

Through a wide variety of written and visual sources from many religious traditions around the world, *Religious Transformations in the Early Modern World* allows students to experience this captivating era of global religious change, one characterized by interactions, reforms, reinvigorations, conversions, and innovations, as well as responses to all of these. This volume includes some sources that have long been regarded as canonical when studying this period, such as Martin Luther's *Freedom of a Christian* and letters between the Ottoman sultan Selim I and the Safavid shah Ismail, and others that rarely appear outside of works for specialists, such as a hymn to the Mexica god Huitzilopochtli and a letter from the female Japanese Christian convert Hosokawa Tama Gracia. It includes works that are actually as well as metaphorically canonical, such as selections from the Guru Granth, the central Sikh sacred text. In addition, the book provides sources that set forth religious doctrines and philosophical ideas, prescribe and depict devotional activities and patterns of behavior, demand dramatic change, and defend long-standing institutions and practices. While some of the sources were written by highly trained scholars for other learned individuals, many others were intended for, and a few written by, ordinary believers.

This book addresses religious transformations in five geographical regions—Mesoamerica, Europe, Africa and Southwest Asia, South Asia, and East Asia. A general introduction to the volume sets out four primary themes that emerge in every geographical region: cross-cultural interactions, the role of authorities and elites, notions of divine and human nature, and ideas about morality and the duties of the believer. Questions posed throughout the volume highlight these themes and encourage students to compare religious developments around the world and investigate ways in which they were connected in the early modern period. Each of the five chapters following the introduction focuses on a single regional case study. To prepare students to read the sources, each chapter begins with an overview of the region and its traditions.

By providing information on a wide range of significant historical trends, this volume encourages the development of skills essential to understanding and applying historical knowledge: reading and analyzing different kinds of evidence, identifying and understanding patterns of continuity and/or change over time, and grasping the interconnectedness of historical developments across cultures. A number of useful pedagogic aids are provided to help students analyze and compare evidence within and across chapters and beyond: The chapter introductions contain thematic questions about the sources that follow; each source begins with a headnote providing background and posing specific questions about that reading or image; and a set of Questions to Consider at the end of the volume encourages students to compare transformations across cultures. A chronology of important events in the regions and religions covered, a selected bibliography, and an index round out the tools to support student exploration of the sources.

ACKNOWLEDGMENTS

This book encourages students to see processes of religious change in this period as linked in complex ways, and in writing it, I, too, had to develop new links, not only relying on the suggestions of close friends and colleagues, but also on the expertise of people I did not know previously, who were unfailingly helpful. For their assistance and suggestions I would like to thank Ellen Amster, Frank Doehringer, Larry Fine, Dina Legall, Aims McGinnis, Leslie Peirce, Kumkum Sangari, Haruko Narata Ward, and Michael Winter, along with the readers for Bedford/St. Martin's who reviewed the manuscript: Angela Feres, Grossmont College; Kris Lane, College of William & Mary; Martin Nesvig, University of Miami; Scott Reese, Northern Arizona University; Gurinder Singh Mann, University of California, Santa Barbara; Karen Spierling, University of Louisville; Samuel Thomas, University of Alabama at Huntsville; Joel Tishken, Columbus State University of Georgia; Katherine Van Lieve, Calvin College; and André Wink, University of Wisconsin. I would also like to thank the editorial staff at Bedford/St. Martin's who assisted with various aspects of the volume's preparation and production: Joan Feinberg, Mary Dougherty, Katherine Meisenheimer, Jane Knetzger, Heidi Hood, Katherine Flynn, Beth Welch, Louise Townsend, Emily Berleth, and Nancy Benjamin of Books By Design. Finally, a special note of thanks to Bonnie Smith, the series editor for world history, who first suggested this project to me.

Merry E. Wiesner-Hanks

A Note about the Text and Translations

In choosing texts for this volume, I tried to pick those that would represent key aspects of transformations within religious traditions as well as interactions among them. Because these transformations involved various processes, including devotional innovations, institutional reforms, theological insights, reassertions of tradition, and even military campaigns, the sources are diverse in genre, style, and tone. Because this volume has a global scope, the texts are also diverse in language and include material that was originally written in eleven different languages or dialects. Some of these sources, such as the Sikh sacred texts or Ignatius Loyola's *Spiritual Exercises*, are important in the spiritual life of millions of people today and have been translated into many of the world's languages in the centuries since they were first written; I have here used what are considered authoritative English translations. Other sources, such as the Mexica hymns, Sahagún's psalms, or al-Maghili's responses, have been translated into English for the first time only recently because of increasing interest by English-language scholars in the practices or developments for which they provide evidence. I have here used these scholarly translations, as I have used scholarly translations for other material from Hebrew, Latin, Spanish, German, Arabic, Hindi, Chinese, and Japanese, including one (from German) that I did myself. A few of the sources, such as Abu'l Fazl's *Akbarnama*, were translated into English more than a century ago, so the style of the translation may seem somewhat old-fashioned; these remain the only English translations that exist, however. I have added explanatory notes and pronunciation guides to the translations where necessary and have provided fuller discussion of many of the texts in the headnotes, especially for those in which the origins or impact of the text illuminates an aspect of religious transformation in this era.

Contents

Illustrations

THE BEDFORD SERIES IN HISTORY AND CULTURE

Religious Transformations in the Early Modern World

A Brief History with Documents

PART ONE

Introduction:
Religious Changes
around the Globe

In the fifteenth and sixteenth centuries, interactions among diverse cultures increased dramatically around the world. Between 1405 and 1423, Chinese treasure fleets under Admiral Zheng He[1] sailed throughout the South China Sea, Indian Ocean, and Arabian Sea on voyages designed to convince people of Chinese power and gain control over foreign trade with China. At about the same time, Prince Henry of Portugal, later dubbed Prince Henry the Navigator, supported Portuguese explorations down the west African coast and military expeditions against Muslim forces in North Africa. Portuguese ships traded with west African empires, and at the end of the fifteenth century Portuguese fleets began to sail profitable sea routes to India. In 1492 the Genoese mariner Christopher Columbus landed on an island in the Caribbean, initiating a series of Spanish voyages that became even more profitable than the Indian routes, and linking the two hemispheres for the first time since the initial prehistoric human migration.

This increased interregional interaction built on developments in the immediately preceding period, such as the expansion of the Mongol Empire and the creation of an extensive Indian Ocean trading network by Arabic, Persian, and Malay merchants. The scale of the new

[1]jun HUH.

1

contacts between peoples was so much greater than what had come before, however, that many historians see the fifteenth century as the beginning of an entirely new era in world history, generally termed *early modern*. The term *early modern*, first used by historians of Europe to describe political, economic, and cultural shifts there, was initially used in world history primarily to denote economic developments.[2] Trade and other economic issues are indeed important factors in the dramatic increase in the level of global interaction that marks the era, but religion was also crucial. Religion both motivated and shaped increased contacts. As one historian of early modern China comments, "elites, ideas, and religions moved across regions with greater frequency than ever before, significantly influencing intellectual and cultural life."[3]

This book provides sources that will allow you to examine religious interactions and other religious changes in many parts of the world in the period from 1450 to 1600. *Religion* is a word we all use regularly, and its meaning may seem self-evident; as one current dictionary defines it, religion is "people's beliefs and opinions concerning the existence, nature, and worship of a deity or deities, and divine involvement in the universe and human life." Yet what religion is and what it is not is often contested. For example, many scholars do not view Confucianism as a religion because it does not teach the worship of a god or gods or have an organized structure; they view it instead as a philosophy or way of life. Many people today, however, also do not worship a specific deity or belong to any organized church and yet still think of themselves as "religious," so in their understanding of what makes something a religion, Confucianism *would* be a religion. Others do view religion primarily as an institutionalized system of beliefs and practices, and if they do not belong to such an institution, they might say, "I'm spiritual, but not religious." In the early modern period, adherents of some religions denied that the beliefs held by other groups were religions at all, judging them instead to be superstitions. Such judgments continue today, when people comment that something "is not really a

---

[2]Some world historians object to the term *early modern* because it seems to imply that there was only one path—that taken by Europe—to modernity, but many have come to use it, although they often explain their reasons for doing so explicitly. How human history is divided into time periods and labeled, a process called *periodization*, is often a topic of discussion and debate in world history.

[3]Evelyn S. Rawski, "The Qing Formation and the Early-Modern Period," in *Qing Formation in World-Historical Time*, ed. Lynn A. Struve (Cambridge, Mass.: Harvard University Press, 2004), 211.

religion, it's just a cult" or make similar statements. This book defines religion very broadly and describes all the traditions it includes as such, but it is important to remember that many of the authors whose words you will read in these pages would not have agreed. This book also describes individuals' religious allegiance generally in terms they themselves used, such as "Christian," "Muslim," or "Sikh." In some cases, their religious opponents would not have agreed that they actually were members of this group. Such hostilities are one of the things we will explore in this book, but we will use people's self-definitions when describing them.

There were many different kinds of religious interactions in the early modern world. Some of these occurred informally. As merchants, sailors, soldiers, bankers, and people of all types seeking their fortunes from many parts of the world came together in port cities, they brought their religious practices and traditions with them. Adherents of different faiths thus lived side by side, and intermarriage created households that were mixed religiously as well as ethnically.

Some interactions were the result of royal interest in religious ideas. In the Mughal[4] Empire, for example, the emperor Akbar (ruled 1556–1605) built a special building where Muslims, Hindus, Zoroastrians, Christians, and scholars of other faiths could discuss their beliefs and practices. A religious innovator himself, he later developed what he termed the "Divine Faith" that combined ideas and rituals from many religions.

Interactions among people of different religious traditions in the early modern period involved violence and domination more often than peaceful discussion, however. The Christian missionaries who accompanied Portuguese and Spanish explorers and conquerors in the Americas, Africa, and Asia often destroyed temples, books, and other objects sacred to indigenous religions and became agents in exploitative colonial governments. Christian rulers in the Iberian peninsula required all Jews to convert or leave in 1492, and at the same time Jews who lived in some North African oasis cities were killed and their synagogues burned down.

Along with interactions in which members of different religions confronted one another, the early modern period saw dramatic changes *within* many religious traditions. For reasons that varied widely, leaders, thinkers, and many ordinary people in the fifteenth and sixteenth centuries determined that changes were needed in religious beliefs and

[4]MOO-guhl.

practices. Some of these thinkers were highly educated and drew on long textual traditions but thought those traditions had become stale and sought to focus on what they viewed as the spiritual core. They reformed existing religions, developed new spiritual practices, and occasionally created new religions. Many religious leaders created new texts or translated existing works so that they were more accessible through oral, written, or sometimes printed versions. Believers in many traditions sought to find the proper balance between acceptance and rejection of older ideas and sacred texts and to define the relationship between the human and the divine in new ways. Once they had settled on the ideas they considered correct, they sought to convert others to their way of thinking, through teaching, persuasion, and, in many places, force.

Reforms and reinvigorations *within* traditions developed at the same time that opportunities for interactions *among* religions were increasing, and these developments played off one another. Religious innovations and reforms shaped subsequent interactions among religions and were shaped by them. To capture this complexity, this book uses the phrase *religious transformations* for all of these interwoven developments: interactions, reforms, reinvigorations, conversions, innovations, and responses to all of these.

RELIGIOUS INNOVATIONS AND REFORMS

Reforms and innovations within a specific religious tradition occurred in many parts of the world in the early modern era. In Mesoamerica, the Mexica[5] official—and half-brother to the emperor—Tlacaélel[6] (1397–1487) promoted expanded worship of the tribal god Huitzilopochtli,[7] created new rituals to honor him, and declared that the Mexica had a special sacred role in history.

In Europe, scholars and ordinary people complained that the western Christian Church, headed by the pope in Rome, was concerned more with wealth and power than with the spiritual needs of believers. Christian humanists such as Desiderius Erasmus[8] (1466–1536) called for reforms, as did many others, including church officials and members of the clergy. One of these was Martin Luther (1483–1546), a

---

[5]meh-SHEE-cah.
[6]tlah-kah-EL-el.
[7]wheet-zee-loh-POHCHT-lee.
[8]deh-seh-DEHR-ee-us eh-RAS-mus.

German monk and university professor, who decided in the early 1520s that the Roman Catholic Church was so corrupt and misguided that it should be rejected rather than reformed. Luther's ideas and those of many of his contemporaries created a movement later termed the *Protestant Reformation* that permanently divided western Christianity. In Spain, Ignatius Loyola[9] (1491?–1556) and Teresa of Avila[10] (1515–1582) also thought that Christianity was in trouble but saw the solution as stricter obedience to the pope and existing practices, not a break from them. By the late sixteenth century, Roman Catholic Christianity was reinvigorated in what came to be called the *Catholic Reformation.*

In south Asia, the spiritual teacher Guru Nanak[11] (1469–1539), living in the Punjab area of what is now the India-Pakistan border, added his own insights to elements of Hinduism, Islam, and other traditions to found what was later called *Sikhism,*[12] a word taken from the Sanskrit word for "learner" or "disciple." In China, the scholar-officials Wang Yangming (1472–1529) and Li Zhi[13] (1527–1602) asserted that reforms were needed in Confucianism and suggested that other religious traditions such as Buddhism or Daoism, or more intensive individual personal meditation, might offer better models for living.

In southwest Asia, Jewish thinkers such as Moses Cordovero[14] (1522–1570) and Isaac Luria[15] (1534–1572) advocated stricter ethical principles based on the teachings of the Kabbalah,[16] a group of mystical texts that offered believers ways of approaching or unifying with God. They created new forms of Kabbalistic practice among communities that included Jewish refugees from zealously Catholic Spain.

Mysticism was also part of the Muslim tradition, particularly in the diverse movement known as Sufism,[17] whose leaders organized brotherhoods of followers that engaged in spiritual and charitable practices. In the mid-fifteenth century, one Sufi brotherhood, that of the Safavids in Iran, became increasingly militant and political. At the end of the century, Ismail (?–1524), a charismatic teenaged boy who was the hereditary leader of the Safavids, assembled an army and proclaimed

[9]ig-NEH-shus loy-OH-lah.
[10]AH-vee-luh.
[11]goo-roo NAH-nock.
[12]SEEK-izm.
[13]lee SHEE.
[14]cohr-doh-VEHR-oh.
[15]LOO-ree-ah.
[16]kah-BAH-lah.
[17]SOO-fizm.

himself ruler, or shah. He also declared that all of his subjects would from that point on accept Shi'ite Islam, setting Iran on a path that has since shaped its history and that of the world.

The Safavids were not the only people whose religious and political concerns were closely linked, for many rulers took the lead in religious changes. At the western end of the Muslim world in West Africa, Askia Muhammad Turé[18] (ruled 1493–1528), later known as "Askia the Great," took over the throne of the Songhay Empire in 1493. He reinvigorated Islam, viewing it as a means of strengthening the Songhay Empire. Askia used Islamic scholars as advisers on legal and political matters, supported the building of mosques, and encouraged the writing of books on Muslim history and law. In Europe, rulers recognized that breaking with the Catholic Church would allow them to confiscate its land and other property and give them authority over religion as well as other aspects of life. The rulers of Denmark, Sweden, Norway, England, Scotland, Poland, and many of the territories within the German Empire accepted Protestant ideas and reformed their states, fully understanding the practical benefits of doing so.

INTERWOVEN TRANSFORMATIONS

These religious innovations and reforms shaped subsequent interactions among religions and were shaped by them, so that processes of religious transformation in the early modern world were often interwoven with one another across greater distances than they had been earlier. There are many examples of this. In Mesoamerica, the sacred role that Tlacaélel envisoned for the Mexica involved human sacrifice, and the Mexica increased their campaigns of war against neighboring groups, for captives were the primary sacrificial victims. When Spanish forces landed in Mesoamerica several decades later, many indigenous groups who had been victimized by this practice allied with the Spanish against the Mexicas, providing the troops that allowed the Spanish leader Hernán Cortés to conquer the Mexica Empire in 1521. Stories of human sacrifice were used as justification for Spanish conquest and provided an additional motivation for Catholic missionaries, who began coming to Mesoamerica, or what came to be called New Spain, very shortly after Cortés's conquest. By the middle

---

[18]AH-skee-ah moo-HAH-med TOO-reh.

of the sixteenth century, members of new religious orders, such as the Jesuits, founded as part of the Catholic Reformation, became particularly active as missionaries, taking Catholic Christianity around the world and claiming millions of converts. (The bulk of Protestant missionary activity came later, in the nineteenth and twentieth centuries.) In the Ottoman Empire, Sultan Süleyman[19] the Magnificent (1494–1566), who was a Sunni Muslim, determined that limited religious diversity would not weaken his empire, and allowed Christians and Jews to maintain their own traditions and leaders. Safavid Shi'ism tested the limits of Süleyman's tolerance, however, because the Ottomans saw all Shi'ites as linked to the Safavid dynasty and thus as political opponents as well as heretics. Ottoman officials arrested and charged people with being Safavid sympathizers, testing their loyalty by demanding they say Sunni prayers. Conversely, Sunni Muslims were persecuted in the Safavid Empire, and hostilities between the Safavid and Ottoman Empires continued for centuries.

In South Asia, people who had formerly been Hindu or Muslim converted to Sikhism, and it eventually became the world's fifth largest text-based religion.[20] Sikhs joined scholars from other religions at the discussions sponsored by Akbar, which may have also included scholars familiar with Confucian reforms in China. In East Asia, traditional Confucian ideas were championed by scholars at the court of the ruler of Japan as well as the emperor of China, though some Japanese thinkers also accepted the more individualistic Confucianism of Wang Yangming. Christian missionaries, primarily Jesuit priests, traveled to China and Japan as well as Akbar's India, where they interacted with Confucian officials, Buddhist monks, and followers of other religious traditions. In China, Christian conversions were limited, but in Japan they may have numbered as many as half a million and eventually provoked a harsh response from the rulers, who otherwise saw their religious heritage as drawing on many traditions.

The early modern period thus saw a huge number of religious transformations, some that came about primarily through the interactions of different cultures and some that developed within cultures but came to shape later interactions. This book provides documents from

---

[19]SOO-lay-man.

[20]Scholars of religion differentiate between religions centered on a sacred text or texts, and those in which beliefs and traditions are primarily communicated orally. Among text-based religions, those with the largest numbers of adherents today are (in order) Christianity, Islam, Hinduism, Buddhism, Sikhism, and Judaism.

many of these transformations. The documents provide information about religious ideas, as well as people's devotional actions and behavior. The book is arranged geographically in five chapters: Mesoamerica, Europe, Africa and Southwest Asia, South Asia, and East Asia. Each chapter introduction includes a historical overview and a discussion of issues related to the sources presented in the chapter. It also includes a brief series of questions about the sources within that chapter. Each source has a headnote describing the author and other important factors about the source. The book ends with a postscript, a chronology, discussion questions, and a selected bibliography.

PRIMARY THEMES

The sources in the book range widely and will allow many lines of analysis and comparison. Four themes are particularly important to the story of religious transformations in this era, however. The first, as you no doubt expect, is interactions, the ways in which adherents of one tradition responded to those of another in this era of religious change. A second theme is the role of authorities and elites in shaping these interactions and innovations. These two themes are common topics in world history, which is at its heart a story of interactions among human groups, often controlled by the elites that hold power. The final two themes are more distinctly religious: The third involves notions of divine and human nature and the fourth ideas about morality and the duties of the believer. Changes and conflicts in ideas about these issues during the early modern period led to violent riots, decades of warfare, persecutions and expulsions, missionary ventures over thousands of miles, and mass and individual conversions. They also led to executions of religious dissidents, which were viewed as martyrdoms by those who agreed with the dissident point of view. People living during this era took religious ideas very seriously, and it is important for us to understand what they viewed as worth killing and dying for.

1. *Interactions.* In many ways every religious transformation in this era was an interaction. Reforms within one religious tradition, such as the Protestant Reformation or Wang Yangming's suggestions for changes in Confucian teachings, set traditional ideas against innovative ones, and set those who supported the old against those who supported the new. Even those who never actually encountered people of

different faiths, such as Teresa of Avila who lived in a convent in Spain, saw their words and actions within the context of interactions with their opponents.

Some of the interactions were violent conflicts in which religion played a significant role, including colonial conquests in Mesoamerica and war between Protestants and Catholics in Europe and between Ottomans and Safavids in southwestern Asia. You will find examples of religious leaders who were deeply hostile to those of other faiths, and perhaps even more hostile toward those who had a different understanding of the same faith. They depicted their enemies or those who disagreed with them in harsh language and unforgiving images.

You will also find examples of interactions that were intentional missionary efforts, as adherents of one faith sought to gain converts among others. Followers of new religions, such as the Sikhs, gained converts by spreading their ideas to those who had formerly been followers of other, older traditions. Catholic missionaries also sought converts among Protestants in Europe, Buddhists in Japan, and followers of the Mexica religion in Mesoamerica. Sometimes conversions were accompanied by violence, but not always. Sometimes attempts at conversion were simply heated discussions among scholars, although such men were no less convinced of the superiority of their ideas than the soldiers who killed their religious opponents. A few of these interactions occurred within an atmosphere of toleration, of which the best-known example was the court of Akbar.

Interaction sometimes resulted in conversion, but it also sometimes resulted in religious synthesis, or the blending of different religious traditions. Akbar's Divine Faith, reformed Confucianism, and Christianity in Mesoamerica are all examples of religious synthesis, in which elements of different traditions are mixed together, and you may find other examples as you read the sources.

2. *The role of authorities and elites.* Religious transformations both enhanced and challenged the role of authorities. Within many traditions, the importance of priests or other religious officials became a matter of debate; some regarded a strong priestly or scholarly group as essential, while others advocated a more individualistic or egalitarian spirituality. This second group stressed that close relations with the divine were not to be limited to an elite group with official positions, but could be achieved by many people through prayer, rituals, and sometimes mystical encounters. Sufism and the Kabbalah both offered believers direct mystical approaches to God, and Teresa

of Avila had visions of Christ and the angels. Mystics often challenged church hierarchies, though not always, and the tension between obedience to authorities and to one's own inner voice can sometimes be found within the writings of a single person.

The proper connections between religion and the state were also debated. Many political leaders in the early modern period thought that it was essential that everyone living within a territory follow the same religious tradition, or at least outwardly conform and not engage in practices that clearly aligned them with a tradition the ruler viewed as unacceptable. Thus worship of Huitzilopochtli was ordered wherever the Mexica conquered, Catholic mass was prohibited in Protestant England, circumcision (a practice of both Jews and Muslims) was outlawed in Catholic Spain, Mexica ceremonies were forbidden in Catholic Mexico, and Jews were forbidden to enter the Muslim Songhay Empire. Those who defied such laws risked penalties imposed by secular political authorities, not simply by religious officials, which could range from fines and confiscation of property to gruesome executions. Not everyone supported the close connections between religion and the state, however. A few Christian missionaries argued that force was never an effective tactic in conversion, and the radical Chinese thinker Li Zhi asserted that state enforcement of ideas would cause people to act worse, not better. The documents in this book will allow you to analyze various roles played by political authorities in religious transformations of this era, as well as the range of opinions about those roles.

3. *Notions of divine and human nature.* Early modern religious writers in many traditions wrestled with issues of divine power. Some authors, such as John Calvin, emphasized the transcendence of divine power and the distance between God or the gods and humans, while others, such as Isaac Luria, emphasized the proximity between believers and aspects of the divine. Religious thinkers in many traditions use similar metaphors and symbols when referring to divine power, including light, fire, and blood.

Ideas about divine power were related to understandings of human nature and will. For Calvin (and others), humans had no power to determine their own fate or anything else about the cosmos, while for Luria (and others) humans had both the power and the responsibility to carry out important spiritual tasks. For some, human nature was basically good, although those who thought this disagreed about whether education improved people's innate understanding or corrupted it. Orthodox

Confucian thinkers in China created a huge system of schools and examinations to train men in Confucian principles, while Li Zhi thought the uneducated mother of one of his students had far more spiritual insight than most scholars. For other religious thinkers, human nature was totally depraved, and no amount of education (or anything else) could change this. The sources in this book provide examples of these widely varying opinions and allow you to see the ways in which they shaped interactions both within and among religious traditions.

4. *Ideas about morality and the duties of the believer.* Reformers in many traditions set out certain duties as incumbent on a believer. They viewed everyday activities and family life as opportunities for people to display religious and moral values, and thus they put a high value on everyday life. At the same time, they also stressed the importance of spiritual over earthly concerns and criticized religious practices if they were done without the proper inward belief or faith. These two issues—life in this world and life directed toward a world to come—could come into conflict, and religious thinkers wrestled with the proper balance between the two. As you will see in the documents in this book, condemnations of other religions sometimes centered on the way this balance was defined. Religious practices and standards of behavior viewed as essential by traditionalists were discounted as unimportant or even harmful by reformers. Adherents of one tradition were actually more often criticized by those of another for their outward practices than for their conceptions of the divine, for these outward practices were easily visible. Conversion from one religion to another was a gradual process in terms of spiritual understanding but was demonstrated by beginning to participate in ceremonies that carried religious meaning. This book includes texts and images used in or depicting such ceremonies, including processions, weddings, and the recitation of chants and prayers.

Religious leaders set out different expectations for men and women, making gender distinctions in terms of spiritual duties and religious practices and establishing standards of ideal masculine and feminine behavior. Almost all of the sources in this book are by male authors— just as are almost all documents from this period in general—but these men do not hesitate to prescribe what women, as well as men, should do to display proper religious devotion. Reformers' ideas about marriage and sexual conduct were linked to their notions of gender and were often an arena of conflict between groups. Protestants, Sikhs, and Confucians all discounted the value of ascetic celibacy and praised married life, while Catholics in Europe and Catholic missionaries in Mexico praised virginity and tried to enforce Christian patterns of marriage.

Debates about the proper role for authorities, the relationship between the human and the divine, the moral duties of the believer, and expected devotional practices for men and women emerge in religious writings from many eras, not just the early modern era. They were thrown in particularly sharp relief in this era, however, because of the increased level of cultural interaction and of internal reform and innovation. "What does God (or the gods, or the heavens) expect of me?" was an especially challenging question when so many different answers presented themselves, sometimes within one's own neighborhood or even within one's own family.

PART TWO

The Documents

1

Mesoamerica: Mexica Innovations
and Mexican Catholicism

BACKGROUND

Mesoamerica saw two dramatic religious developments in the early
modern era, both of them the result of military conquests. In the fifteenth century, the Mexica Empire expanded, and the royal official
Tlacaélel linked its military victories to the worship of Huitzilopochtli,
declaring that the Mexicas had a special sacred role in history. In the
sixteenth century, Spanish forces conquered the Mexicas and other
Mesoamerican peoples, and demanded that existing religious practices cease and everyone become Christian. The Spanish, too, viewed
their victories as signs that they were favored by God.

Mexica religious innovations were related to earlier political and
religious developments. Around 1300, a group of Nahuatl-speaking[1]
people are believed to have migrated southward from what is now
northern Mexico, settling on the shores and islands in Lake Texcoco
in the central valley of Mexico. Here they built the twin cities of
Tenochtitlán[2] and Tlatelolco,[3] which by 1500 were probably larger
than any city in Europe except Istanbul. As they migrated, these
people conquered many neighboring city-states and established an
empire. This empire was later termed the *Aztec Empire* and the people
called the *Aztecs*. The name was not used at the time, however, and
now most scholars prefer the term *Mexica* to refer to the empire and
its people. (The Mexica spoke Nahuatl, as did other groups, and the
peoples of the central valley of Mexico and some neighboring regions
are also referred to as Nahua.) The Mexica rulers demanded regular
tribute of goods and laborers from other native peoples they conquered. War came to be seen as a religious duty to the Mexicas,

[1] nuh-WAT-tul.
[2] ten-OACH-teet-LAHN.
[3] tlah-te-LOH-ko.

15

through which nobles, and occasionally commoners, honored the gods, gained prestige, and often acquired wealth.

The Mexicas worshipped a number of gods and goddesses, as well as some deities that had dual natures as both male and female. The basic conflict in the world was understood as one between order and disorder, though the proper life balanced these two, as disorder could never be completely avoided. Disorder was linked to dirt and uncleanness, so temples, shrines, and altars were kept very clean; Nahua rituals of purification often involved sweeping or bathing. Like many polytheists, Mexicas took the deities of people they encountered into their own pantheon, or mixed their attributes with those of existing gods. Quetzalcoatl,[4] for example, the feathered serpent god found among many Mesoamerican groups, was generally revered by the Mexicas as a creator deity and source of knowledge; opposing him were gods of death and the underworld. (See Document 1.) Among the deities venerated by Mexica and other Mesoamerican groups was Huitzilopochtli, a young warrior god whose name translates fully as "Blue Hummingbird of the South" (or "on the Left"). Huitzilopochtli was conceived when his goddess mother Coatlicue[5] picked up a mysterious ball of feathers that fell from the sky; he dressed in warrior's clothing and killed most of his siblings the moment he was born, establishing himself as a fierce and powerful opponent.

Huitzilopochtli was originally a somewhat ordinary god of war and of young men, but in the fifteenth century he became the Mexicas' most important deity. (See Document 2.) This change was primarily the work of Tlacaélel, the very long-lived chief adviser to several Mexica emperors. Tlacaélel first gained influence during wars in the 1420s in which the Mexicas defeated the rival Tepanecs. He advised the emperor that new histories were needed in which the destiny of the Mexica people was made clearer. Older historical texts were destroyed, and in these new chronicles the fate of the Mexicas was directly connected to Huitzilopochtli. Mexica writing was primarily pictographic, drawn and then read by specially trained scribes, who used written records as an aid to oral presentation, especially for legal issues, historical chronicles, religious and devotional poetry, and astronomical calculations.

According to these new texts, the Mexicas had been guided by Huitzilopochtli to Lake Texcoco, where they saw an eagle perched on a cactus, which a prophecy had told would mark the site of their new city. Huitzilopochtli kept the world alive by bringing the Sun's

[4]ket-sahl-KOHT-uhl.
[5]koh-AHT-lee-kew.

warmth, but to do this he required the Mexicas, who increasingly saw themselves as the "people of the Sun," to provide a steady offering of human blood. (See Document 3.) The worship of Huitzilopochtli became linked to cosmic forces as well as daily survival. In Nahuatl tradition, the universe was understood to exist in a series of five Suns, or five cosmic Ages. Four Ages had already passed and their Suns had been destroyed; the Fifth Sun, the Age in which the Mexicas were now living, would also be destroyed unless the Mexicas fortified the Sun with the energy found in blood. Warfare thus not only brought new territory under Mexica control, but it also provided sacrificial victims for their collaboration with divine forces. With these ideas, Tlacaélel created what one leading contemporary scholar of Nahuatl religion and philosophy has termed a "mystico-militaristic" conception of Mexica destiny. (See Documents 4 and 5.)

Human sacrifice was practiced in many cultures of Mesoamerica, including among the Yucatec Maya and the Inca as well as the Mexica, before the changes introduced by Tlacaélel, but the number of victims is believed to have increased dramatically during the last period of Mexica rule. A huge pyramid-shaped temple in the center of Tenochtitlán, dedicated to Huitzilopochtli and the water god Tlaloc, was renovated and expanded many times, the last in 1487. Each expansion was dedicated by priests sacrificing war captives. Similar ceremonies were held regularly throughout the year on days dedicated to Huitzilopochtli, attended by many observers, including representatives from neighboring states as well as masses of Mexicas. According to many accounts, victims were placed on a stone slab and their hearts cut out with an obsidian knife; the officiating priest then held the heart up as an offering to the Sun.

Estimates about the number of people sacrificed to Huitzilopochtli and other Mexica gods vary enormously and are impossible to verify. Both Mexica and later Spanish accounts clearly exaggerated the numbers, but most historians today assume that between several hundred and several thousand people were killed each year. In some years it was difficult to provide this many war captives, so that other types of people, including criminals, slaves, and people supplied as tribute, were sacrificed as well. Such victims did not have the same status as captives, however, and Mexicas engaged in special wars, termed *flower* (or *flowery*) *wars*, simply to provide victims for sacrifices. Flowers were frequently associated metaphorically with warfare in Nahuatl culture, with blood described as a flower of warfare, swords and banners as blooming like flowers, and a warrior's life as fleeting like a flower's blooming. (See Documents 3 and 4.) The objective of flower wars was to capture warriors from the other side, not kill them.

Mexica demands for tribute in goods and people led to great resentment on the part of many other groups and enhanced resistance to further Mexica expansion. Tlaxcala,[6] a loosely organized confederation of several hundred towns southeast of Tenochtitlán, resisted Mexica conquest despite a trade blockade and threats of massive flower wars. In 1519, the Spanish conquistador Hernán Cortés, with several hundred men, arrived in Tlaxcala. He was initially opposed by Tlaxcalteca troops, but many of them were killed by Cortés's forces. The Tlaxcaltecans decided to ally with Cortés, and a combined force of several hundred Spanish soldiers and sailors, several hundred Native Americans and Africans from the Caribbean, and several thousand Tlaxcaltecans marched northward toward Tenochtitlán.

The Mexica emperor Moctezuma[7] II initially greeted Cortés and his allies and allowed them into the city, but the Spanish were expelled by force when some of Cortes's men massacred Mexica priests at the temple of Huitzilopochtli. A second battle in 1521, after the Spanish had gained more allies and after much of Tenochtitlán's population had died of smallpox, brought by Spanish troops, ended in a Spanish/Tlaxcaltecan victory. Cortés did not fulfill the agreement he had made with the Tlaxcaltecans to allow them to rule Tenochtitlán, and, like other indigenous groups, they soon were required to pay tribute to the Spanish instead of the Mexicas.

Tlacaélel's reforms were a minor change compared to the dramatic transformations that followed Spanish conquest. The papacy granted special privileges—the *patronato*—to the Spanish crown to control almost all aspects of religious life in its colonies. Colonial forces included Catholic missionaries who worked to convert indigenous people and to establish churches and church institutions for immigrants. The first missionaries, a group of twelve Franciscan friars, arrived in the area conquered by Cortés in 1524, and members of other Catholic orders followed. They initially preached to indigenous people in Spanish, which few understood, and some missionaries began to learn native languages, including Nahuatl, sometimes first learning a sermon by heart that had been translated by an interpreter, then expanding their understanding to be able to preach and teach on their own. Following a pattern that had allowed Christianity to spread

[6]tlahcks-KAH-lah.
[7]MOHK-teh-ZOO-mah.

in Europe from the fourth through the twelfth centuries, they often first converted members of the elite, hoping they would convince more ordinary people to convert as well. The Franciscans opened a school for boys from noble Mexica families designed to train an indigenous clergy, teaching them Spanish and Latin as well as Christian doctrine.

Some missionaries were idealistic, seeing the New World as a place to plant Christianity anew, away from what they saw as the hopeless corruption of European culture. However, they also viewed the destruction of Mexica religion as a necessary part of their mission. Ceremonies were banned and religious statuary smashed. Temples and other sacred buildings were pulled down on orders of the Spanish colonial government, with those to Huitzilopochtli often the first to be destroyed. Catholic shrines or churches were erected on the sites of Mexica temples. Books of Nahuatl picture-writing were burned by Spanish soldiers, officials, and clergy, who could not read them but still considered them "picture-books of the Devil."

Missionaries initially hoped simply to transplant Christian beliefs and practices from Spain to New Spain, but Nahua concepts of human nature, purity, good and evil, order and chaos, the relationship between the soul and the body, time, and many other issues were very different from those in European Christianity. Many missionaries came to recognize that to be effective, they would need to understand native beliefs and to present Christian teachings in ways that would make sense to native peoples. Friars such as Bernardino de Sahagún (1499–1590) began to record information about local beliefs and practices. Within decades after the conquest, missionaries and converts preached regularly in Nahuatl and other indigenous languages. (See Document 6.) They adapted the Roman script used in Europe to create a phonetic version of written Nahuatl. Despite official prohibition of vernacular translations of the Bible, missionaries translated Christian devotional works, including parts of the Bible, into Nahuatl. They wrote new hymns, prayers, explanations of church doctrine, and religious plays. (See Documents 7 and 8.)

Along with explaining the theological and spiritual concepts central to Christianity, missionaries also attempted to persuade—or force— possible converts to adopt Christian practices of marriage, sexual morality, and day-to-day behavior. In many areas, once one was baptized, following Christian patterns in terms of one's marriage rituals and personal demeanor became a more important mark of conversion than understanding the Trinity or other aspects of Christian doctrine. (See Document 8.) St. Joseph, the husband of the Virgin Mary and foster-father of Jesus, was named as the patron saint of New Spain in 1555 and praised as a model convert and model man: a strong protector of his family who controlled his sexual activity. (In Catholic doctrine, Joseph is understood to have remained a virgin.) To enhance Christian practice, missionaries established confraternities—groups of men and women who were not members of the clergy—dedicated to specific saints or devotional practices. (See Document 9.)

Many people resisted Christian teachings and continued to practice their original faith, but far more became Christian. This process used to be described as a "spiritual conquest," in which indigenous beliefs and practices were largely wiped out through force and persuasion. The spread of Catholic Christianity is now viewed very differently, not simply as conquest and resistance—though it was that—but as a process of cultural negotiation and synthesis, during which Christian ideas and practices were accepted but also transformed. (A similar transformation had accompanied the spread of Christianity from the Mediterranean into central and northern Europe between the third and the eighth centuries, as Celtic and Germanic customs were incorporated into Christianity.) In the Americas, this synthesis and transformation involved indigenous people and missionaries, and also slaves, migrants, and people of mixed-race background (*mestizos*), who constituted a larger share of the Mexican population with each generation.

Missionaries themselves made use of similarities. Though they had different connotations, blood and sacrifice were central elements in both Nahua and Christian belief; missionaries could thus explain Jesus's death as a parallel to Mexica sacrifices and illustrate their teaching with images of Jesus bleeding or with his heart on fire. They replaced the Mesoamerican celebration honoring departed ancestors with All Souls' Day, November 2. Converts also transformed ideas and practices. Numerous Catholic saints had specific qualities or stories associated with their lives that paralleled those of Nahua deities, which made their veneration easier. St. John the Baptist, for example, was associated with water and acquired some of the qualities earlier attributed to Tlaloc, the Nahua god of rain. Through this, John the Baptist in Mexico became a slightly different figure than he was in Catholic Europe. Altars to the saints in people's homes in Mexico were swept in the same way that those to Nahua gods had been, which was not the case in Europe.

In the sixteenth and seventeenth centuries, some Christian religious authorities objected to such mixtures, arguing that they brought pagan practices into Christianity in inappropriate ways. Such objections were not very effective, however. All Souls' Day, a relatively minor Christian holiday in Europe, grew more important as the Day of the Dead (*Día de los Muertos*) and continues to be a major feast day (and now public holiday) in Mexico. People visit cemeteries, decorate graves, honor deceased family members with small gifts, and prepare special foods, such as skulls made of sugar or bread dough, strikingly similar to images that had adorned the temples of Mexica deities.

DOCUMENTS

Sources relating to the religion of the Mexica and other Nahua peoples before the Spanish conquest are very rare. Indigenous writing in Mesoamerica was largely pictorial, though it also included symbols linguists call *glyphs* that stood for certain things, such as days. Pictographic documents were produced and read by specially trained scholars, who used them as an aid to oral presentation, especially for legal issues, historical chronicles, and poetry. Most preconquest manuscripts were destroyed by the Spanish, who thought they were demonic, but Nahua scribes continued the tradition of pictorial writing into the seventeenth century, sometimes adding Nahuatl text written in Roman letters, sometimes Spanish or Latin text, or sometimes all of these.

Some of these bilingual texts were written at the behest of Spanish missionaries and some by missionaries themselves. They were often based on earlier pictorial manuscripts that have now been lost, as well as interviews with native people, and frequently include Nahua hymns and other sorts of sacred literature, descriptions of ceremonies and rituals, calendars, and chronicles of historical events. Because they were written or overseen by European Christians or by Nahua converts to Christianity, however, scholars debate to what degree they represent authentic Nahua beliefs, and it is important to keep the Christian perspective of their authors in mind as you read them. The Nahua religious texts they contain are generally viewed as reliable by scholars, however. In fact, many of these books were not published until the nineteenth century because Catholic authorities in Mexico and Spain thought they were *too* reliable and that having access to their histories and religious traditions in these cross-cultural dialogues might encourage people to continue or revert to their "idolatrous" practices.

By contrast to the scarcity of sources about pre-Hispanic religious beliefs, the emergence of a distinctively Mexican Christianity in the sixteenth century has left many traces. Some of these are records of the different ways missionaries attempted to teach indigenous people about Catholic Christianity: collections of sermons, explanations of doctrine that were read out loud, manuals used by priests when they performed religious services or heard confessions, books of catechism, scripts of plays, and written versions of songs and poems. These are generally attributed to Europeans, but these men often worked with multilingual native converts. Again it is difficult to separate the native and the imported voice, as each side influenced the other in a cross-cultural dialogue.

Not everyone supported translations or the creation of materials in Nahuatl or other indigenous languages. Many royal and church officials confiscated and banned not only materials about pre-Hispanic Mexica history, but anything written in Nahuatl. In 1577 the Mexican Catholic Church reaffirmed the prohibition of vernacular translations of the Bible, and some of the devotional works written in Nahuatl have never been published in any language, but remain simply manuscripts.

As you examine these documents, note the central themes: interactions, the role of elites, ideas about divine and human power, and the duties of the believer. What role does devotion to Huitzilopochtli play in shaping interactions between the Mexica and their neighbors? Documents 2 and 7 are hymns or songs, which are important means of expressing religious devotion in many traditions. How do they portray divine or holy figures? Divine power is portrayed in Documents 1, 2, 3, and 8. How does this differ in the Mexica and Christian materials? How is it the same? What other qualities do these sources ascribe to deities? Documents 2, 3, 4, and 7 discuss religious duties of the believer to God or the gods; what parallels can you see? The Catholic materials were produced in order to win converts, so effective preachers and missionaries used references that made sense in Mexica culture. What examples do you find of concepts or images from Documents 2–5 re-emerging in Documents 6–10? In what ways are they different in the new Christian context; in other words, how are they a synthesis of Mexica and Catholic beliefs? How would you compare the Christian religious activities described in Document 10 with Mexica ceremonies as described in Documents 4 and 5? (For questions that relate these documents to those in other chapters in the book, see p. 163.)

1

Gods of Life and Death from The Codex Borgia
ca. 1500

The Codex Borgia, *one of the few surviving painted books from Meso-america before the Spanish conquest, was probably painted in an area south of the Mexica Empire, where people worshipped many of the same gods that the Mexicas did. (No preconquest Mexica books survive at all,*

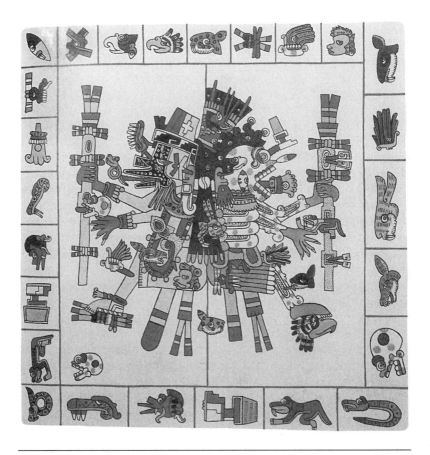

Gisela Díaz and Alan Rodgers, *The Codex Borgia* (New York: Dover Publications, 1993), plate 56.

and the total from all of present-day Mexico is about fifteen.) This page shows Quetzalcoatl, the feathered serpent god of life and wind, sitting back-to-back with Mictlantecuhtli,[1] the god of death and the underworld, framed by twenty signs that stand for various days. How is the idea of balance between opposites, which was central in Mesoamerican culture, conveyed? How do life and death relate to one another in this image?

[1] mihk-lahn-tuh-COOT-lee.

2

Hymn to Huitzilopochtli from the Codices Matritenses

ca. 1550

Huitzilopochtli was honored in many ceremonies, rituals, poems, and hymns. This hymn appears in the Codices Matritenses, two books that are sixteenth-century transcriptions of Nahuatl texts of indigenous elders interviewed by the Spanish Franciscan missionary Bernardino de Sahagún. Sahagún interviewed older men, asking about the culture, songs, doctrines, and history they had learned in Mexica schools before the Spanish conquest and was satisfied that their answers represented authentic Mexica traditions. In the first two lines of this hymn, the singer calls on the god, who answers in the second two lines, asserting his cosmic role. How is Huitzilopochtli praised in the rest of the hymn? What are Mexica men urged to do in his name?

> Huitzilopochtli, the young warrior,
> who acts above! He follows his path!
> "Not in vain did I dress myself in yellow plumes,
> for I am he who has caused the sun to rise."

Miguel León-Portilla, *Mexica Thought and Culture: A Study of the Ancient Nahuatl Mind*, translated from the Spanish by Jack Emory Davis (Norman: University of Oklahoma Press, 1963), 161–62.

You, ominous lord of the clouds,
one is your foot!
The inhabitants of the cold region of wings,
Your hand opens.

Near the wall of the region of heat,
feathers were given, they are scattering.
The war cry was heard . . . Ea, ea!
My god is called the Defender of men.

Oh, now he moves on, he who is dressed in paper,
he who inhabits the region of heat; in the region of dust,
he whirls about in the dust.

Those of Amantla[1] are our enemies;
come and join me!
With struggle is war made;
come and join me!

Those of Pipiltlan[2] are our enemies;
come and join me!
With struggle is war made;
come and join me!

[1]*Amantla*: A town outside the Aztec Empire.
[2]*Pipiltlan*: Another town.

3

Mexica War Songs

1560s

These songs are included in a sixteenth-century manuscript in Nahuatl, later called the Colección de Cantares Mexicanos. *The first song calls on the Sun to rise again and offers the arrows and shields of Tenochtitlán to assist in this. The second song also praises the Sun as the giver of life*

Miguel León-Portilla, *Pre-Columbian Literatures of Mexico*, translated from the Spanish by Grace Lobanov and the author (Norman: University of Oklahoma Press, 1969), 87–88.

and describes a battle in one of the "flower wars" that provided victims for Mexica sacrifices. How do the songs glorify warriors and battle?

From where the eagles are resting,
from where the tigers are exalted,
the Sun is invoked.

Like a shield that descends,
so does the Sun set.
In Mexico night is falling,
war rages on all sides.

Oh Giver of Life!
war comes near. . . .

Proud of itself
is the city of Mexico-Tenochtitlán.
Here no one fears to die in war.
This is our glory.
This is Your Command,
oh Giver of Life!
Have this in mind, oh princes,
do not forget it.
Who could conquer Tenochtitlán?
Who could shake the foundation of heaven?

With our arrows,
with our shields,
the city exists.
Mexico-Tenochtitlán remains.

There is a clamor of bells,
the dust rises as if it were smoke.
The Giver of Life is gratified.
Shield flowers open their blossoms,
the glory spreads,
it becomes linked to earth.
Death is here among the flowers
in the midst of the plain!
Close to the war,
when the war begins,

in the midst of the plain,
the dust rises as if it were smoke,
entangled and twisted round
with flowery strands of death.
Oh Chichimec[1] princes!
Do not fear, my heart!
In the midst of the plain
my heart craves death
by the obsidian edge.
Only this my heart craves:
death in war. . . .

[1] *Chichimec* (chih-CHIH-mek): Name given to peoples of northern Mexico by the Mexica.

4

DIEGO DURÁN

The History of the Indies of New Spain

ca. 1580

The authors of most Nahuatl songs and hymns are unknown, so that it is difficult to trace the activities of Tlacaélel or anyone else from the songs themselves. For that we must turn to annals and histories. One of these is The History of the Indies of New Spain *written in Spanish by the Dominican friar Diego Durán (ca. 1537–1588). Durán came to New Spain as a child, learned Nahuatl, and preached in native villages after joining the Dominican order. His several books on Mexica history and traditions rely on Mexica pictorial records—which he may have been able to interpret himself—as well as interviews and earlier texts by other missionaries. Durán includes speeches by Tlacaélel and others; in including*

Fray Diego Durán, *Mexicas: The History of the Indies of New Spain*, translated, with notes, by Doris Heyden and Fernando Horcasitas (New York: Orion Press, 1964), 91–92, 99–102, 140–42, 202–3.

these, he followed a pattern common among European historians since the time of the ancient Greeks, but he may have actually learned the speeches from native scholars who had memorized them. In the first speech in this excerpt, which begins "Do not sorrow," Tlacaélel compares the "flower wars" to marketplaces in which the Mexicas buy food for Huitzilopochtli through their own blood; only the flesh of fellow Nahuatl-speaking groups, and not that of more distant tribes, will please the god. How does Tlacaélel see the relationship between religion and Mexica political power? What does he see as the religious duties of Mexica men? The final speech is a prayer of Mexica women. How does their role in Mexica devotion to Huitzilopochtli compare to that of men? What evidence do you see in this text of Durán's Christian perspective?

For twelve or thirteen years, during the reign of Huehue Moteczoma [Moctezuma I], there was peace and tranquillity. As he was served and obeyed by all the neighboring cities, he determined to build the temple of his god Huitzilopochtli, like the great king Solomon who, having made peace with all the land, beloved by all the monarchs of the earth and aided by them, built the temple of Jerusalem.

Moteczoma gathered his council and told them his will in the following words: "Lords and chieftains of my kingdom, my heart tells me that I must construct a most sumptuous house to honor our god Huitzilopochtli. You know that he does not yet have a home, even though all of you have dwelling places. Yet he should be the first."

Having obtained approval from Tlacaélel and the council for the building of the temple, the king proposed that messengers be sent to Azcapotzalco, Coyoacan, Xochimilco, Cuitlahuac, Mizquic, Colhuacan and Texcoco, asking that laborers and materials such as lime, stone and wood be sent immediately.

"Powerful lord," protested Tlacaélel, "it would be more proper for you to use your royal authority to the full and treat your vassals as a master and supreme monarch. Every time messengers are sent they are chosen from among the nobility. Where will we find enough noblemen to act as messengers? Remember also that it is a heavy task for them. It would be more fitting if all the rulers, without exception, were brought before you. Standing in your presence, they would then receive your command to build the temple of our god."

Moteczoma agreed with this advice, saying, "Forgive me, lords; even though I am king I sometimes commit errors. That is why it is good that you aid me, giving me advice on things of importance to our city. Let the authorities be called immediately."

When the lords had arrived in Mexico they were brought into the presence of Moteczoma and he spoke to them in this manner: "O sovereigns of Texcoco, Xochimilco, Colhuacan, Cuitlahuac, Mizquic, Coyoacan, Azcapotzalco and Tacuba: You have been brought here because I wish you to consider that our god Huitzilopochtli, father and mother of all, under whose protection we stand, has no dwelling place where he can be worshipped. We have decided to build a sumptuous temple dedicated to his name and to our other gods. You well know you are obliged to serve him and I command you that as soon as you return to your cities you order your vassals to come to this work bringing the necessary materials of stone, lime and wood. All of this will redound to your honor and happiness. Let there be no negligence; let every man put his shoulder to the task so that it can be finished quickly."

"O masters," they answered, "and you especially, ruler of all the land, you who are obeyed by all, whose city stands in a marsh, in the midst of the reeds and the rushes: care for your health and your life; preserve them. We have heard your command and it will be done as well as possible, since it is our duty to obey in all things. Let this work be done for our lord in whose shade and protection we live and take refuge. Decide what is necessary and it will be brought to you."

The king and his men thanked them, being grateful for the good will they had shown. The king ordered them to bring heavy stone for the foundation and light stone for the building, together with lime and wood. And this was done. . . .

News came to Mexico that the people of Tepeaca had murdered a number of Aztec, Texcocan and Tecpanec merchants who had been trading in that city. All of their merchandise had been stolen from them and their bodies thrown to the wild animals.

Moteczoma informed Tlacaélel and all the important Aztec chieftains of these events, stating that he desired to capture the rulers of Tepeaca, bring them to Mexico and give them a cruel death. Tlacaélel, however, answered that this was not sufficient punishment and that it would be better to prepare for war and to destroy them mercilessly. . . .

I am told that the people of Tepeaca did not fight or defend themselves since they felt their resistance would be futile, and in a cowardly way they allowed themselves to be killed like wild animals. Coyolcue, the chieftain, weeping bitterly, crossed his arms and prostrated himself before the Aztecs, begging for mercy. . . .

Tepeaca was now a vassal of the Aztecs and promised to be a perpetual tributary, paying in maize, chilli, salt, pumpkin seeds, cloth, sandals, palm leaf mats, and deerskins. The Tepeacans also promised to provide labor, as carriers on the roads and as workmen to build huts and set up tents in war. They later offered slaves for the abominable sacrifice made to the idols. . . .

When all the prisoners arrived, the priests threw incense into the braziers and incensed the future victims, since they belonged to the gods. Then the priests called Tecuacuiltin (which means "Gods," or "Images of Gods") arrived and broke pieces of maize bread, which were kept in the temples strung on cords, and offered them to the captives. The priests then addressed the prisoners in the following way:

"We welcome you
To this city of Mexico Tenochtitlán
Which is in the great pool of water,
Where the eagle sang and the snake hissed!
Where the fishes fly,
Where the blue waters came out to join the red waters!
Here among the reeds, here among the rushes,
Where reigns the god Huitzilopochtli.
Do not think that you have come here to live;
You have come here to die,
To offer your chests and your throats to the knife.
Only in this way, through your deaths, has it been your fortune
To know this great city.
We salute you and comfort you with these words:

You have not come here because of weakness,
But because of your manliness.
You will die here but your fame will live forever." . . .

[Work on the temple to Huitzilopochtli resumed.]
Soon after this the Aztecs set out to punish the rebellious people of Oaxaca and after having vanquished them they brought back great numbers of victims for sacrifice. The priests of Mexico came out to meet them with incense burners in their hands, intoning hymns to their god. They offered incense to the prisoners, telling them of their fate and giving flowers and tobacco to all. The prisoners set up a frightful wail, shrieking and screaming. It was enough to horrify one.

When Moteczoma proposed that the victims be sacrificed in the new temple, Tlacaélel objected, saying that the building had not been entirely finished, that many statues were incomplete and that the shining mirror which was to represent the sun had not been made.

"Do not sorrow, O lord," said Tlacaélel. "Let it be finished first!
There is time for everything. If you wish it so, let these warriors,
Children of the sun, be sacrificed; but remember
That we will never lack victims for the dedication.
Our god will not be made to wait until new wars arrive.
He will find a way, a market place where he will go
To buy victims, men for him to eat. They will be in his sight.
Like maize cakes hot from the griddle ready for him who wishes to eat.
Let our people, let our army go to this market place!
Let us buy with our blood, our heads and hearts and with our lives,
Precious stones, jade and feathers for our wondrous Huitzilopochtli.
This market place will be situated in Tlaxcala,
Huexotzinco, Cholula, Atlixco, Tliliuhquitepec and Tecoac,
Because if we place it in remote lands such as Yopitzinco,
Michoacan, the land of the Huaxtecs, or on either coast, it will be
    difficult.
Our god does not like the flesh of those barbarous peoples.
They are yellowish, hard, tasteless breads in his mouth.
They are savages and speak strange tongues.
Therefore our market place must be in these six cities.
They will come like warm breads, soft, tasty, straight from the
    fire.". . .

At this time, certain Aztec merchants were killed by the rulers of
the province of Tehuantepec. The Aztec army set out with its provisions, such as toasted grains of corn, maize flour, bean flour, crisp
toasted tortillas, tamales baked in the sun, great loads of chilli, cakes
of ground cacao, all of this in great quantities. Apart from the supplies
provided by the rulers from their great bins and storehouses, each
soldier carried on his back his own food, as much as he could. He
went along with his sword, shield, and other weapons tied to his load,
and with the latter he augmented the ordinary rations that were given
to him.

    While their husbands were gone the wives prayed for them in the
following way:

"O Great Lord of All Things, remember your servant
Who has gone to exalt your honor and the greatness of your name.
He will offer blood in that sacrifice which is war.
Behold, Lord, that he did not go out to work for me
Or for his children! He did not abandon us to obtain things

To support his home, with his tump line on his head,
Or with his digging stick in his hand. He went for your sake,
In your name, to obtain glory for you. Therefore, O Lord,
Let your pious heart have pity on him, who with great labor
And affliction now goes through the mountains and valleys,
Hills and precipices, offering you the moisture from his brow,
His sweat. Give him victory in this war so that he may return
To rest in his home and so that my children and I may see
His countenance again and feel his presence."

This prayer was recited every day at dawn by the women until their sons or husbands, brothers or other relatives, returned.

Ahuitzotl[1] gave orders that in this war all prisoners be slaughtered and that no one bother to take captives since there was much work of conquest to be done and the distance from those provinces to the city of Mexico was great. And so this was a war of slaughter.

[1]*Ahuitzotl* (ah-weets-OH-tel): Mexica emperor (1486–1502).

5

CHIMALPAHIN

Annals

early 1600s

The history of the Mexica Empire is found in works written in Nahuatl as well as Spanish. Domingo Francisco (1579–1660), an ambitious in-digenous young man from southern Mexico, took a position as a minor Catholic official and copyist in Mexico City and began writing chronicles covering Mexica history before and after conquest as well as events that occurred during his own lifetime. He gave himself a more elab-orate title, Domingo Francisco de San Antón Muñon Chimalpahin Quauhtlehuanitzin, taking the last two names from earlier Mexica lords

5a: Rémi Siméon, ed., translated by Jeffrey Merrick, *Annales de Domingo Francisco de San Antón Muñon Chimalpahin Quauhtlehuanitzin* (Paris: Leclerc, 1889), 106–7.
5b: *Codex Chimalpahin: Volume 1*, edited and translated by Arthur J. O. Anderson and Susan Schroeder (Norman: University of Oklahoma Press, 1997), 43, 45, 47, 49.

from his home province; since then he has been generally known as Chimalpahin.[1] *Drawing on chronicles by earlier native authors, histories written by Spanish missionaries, and oral interviews, Chimalpahin wrote the most extensive history of Mexico by a known native author that still survives today, along with other works. What role does Chimalpahin see Tlacaélel and his religious changes playing in creating the Mexica state?*

5a. Itzcóatl, sovereign of Tenochtitlán . . . made war with the assistance especially of his nephew Tlacaélel. They subjected the Azcaputzalcas, the Cuyohuaques, the Xochimilcas and the inhabitants of Cuitlahuacan. It was Tlacaélel who first fought valiantly and with success. Then he never sought to rule in the city of Tenochtitlán, but he governed nobly, lived in abundance, and was content. Then five other great monarchs ruled in Mexico-Tenochtitlán: Moctezuma I, Axayacatl, Tiçocic, Ahuitzotl, and Moctezuma II, under whom the Spaniards arrived. They were very great kings who made themselves feared everywhere, but the one who was the most courageous, the most famous in the state was the great captain, the great warrior Tlacaélel, as will be seen in the annals [that follow]. It was also he who knew how to make the devil Huitzilopochtli into the supreme god of the Mexicans, for he knew how to persuade them.

5b. So great and so many were the achievements and deeds of this man Tlacaeleltzin[2] that it seems as difficult for me to reduce them to brevity as to write and tell about them. As to treating of them with some dispatch and brevity, however, because he was the beginning and foundation of this edifice, it will be necessary to extend and expand [their treatment] more than that of matters ahead [of us]. Among the great achievements of this incomparable man Tlacaeleltzin that may be told of, in my opinion the greatest of all and the one that most arouses my admiration is that this man had the spirit and daring to think of and then undertake and in the end succeed in making [himself and Itzcoatzin] lords of the Mexican people and republic, mistress and subduer of the greater and best part of all the New World, and of as much as [that nation] had been able to subdue and conquer in three hundred and eighty-five years (for such, and even a little more, was the length of time that had elapsed since the founding of

[1] CHEE-mahl-PA-hin.
[2] *Tlacaeleltzin:* Tlacaélel.

Mexico until Tlacaeleltzin cihuacoatl took over the republic); three hundred and three years under captains general, and then sixty-two under government by kings. This was indeed a very short space of time to form and conquer as great an empire as the one the Mexicans had achieved when the cihuacoatl Tlacaeleltzin converted it from a free commonwealth to the rulership of one. It was without doubt the greatest in both size and power of any that the New World had seen or that men had achieved. Such do all the ancient Mexican authors and truthful histories affirm and attest.

6

BERNARDINO DE SAHAGÚN

Sermons

1540

Bernardino de Sahagún[1] *traveled widely, preached sermons, translated parts of the Bible, and wrote prayers, hymns, and devotional texts. In 1540 he wrote out a series of sermons in Nahuatl, which he edited and revised over the next twenty years. He later added an introductory note: "The following are some Sunday and Saints' Day sermons in Nahuatl. They were not translated from any sermonary but rather composed afresh to the measure of the Indians' capacity: brief in subject matter, in congruous language, graceful and straightforward, easy to understand for any who should hear them, high and low, lords and commoners, men and women." In the sermons, Sahagún describes the benefits of heaven for those who converted, but also the pains of hell for those who did not. His portrayal of hell includes features drawn from the European tradition, such as fire, and from Mexica traditions, such as dirt. The shape-shifting creatures who inhabit hell have features that can be found in the descriptions of Mexica deities that Sahagún collected. Placing them in*

[1]behr-nah-DEE-noh deh SAH-hah-gun.

Louise M. Burkhart, *The Slippery Earth: Nahua-Christian Moral Dialogue in Sixteenth-Century Mexico* (Tucson: University of Arizona Press, 1989), 54, 55.

hell made this destination familiarly horrendous to Mexica hearers of the sermon and also transformed native gods into demons, thus incorporating them as lesser—but still very dangerous—figures in Christian theology. Why might this incorporation of Mexica deities and other aspects of indigenous religion have made these sermons unacceptable to Catholic authorities?

Your desert is just pain in *mictlan*.[2] It is very frightening, for worms will eat you, in the fire you will burn, the *tlatlacatecolo*[3] will squeeze you and rend you with metal. You will lie in darkness, in gloom, you will be tied with chains, you will lie crying out tearfully, you will be thirsty, you will be hungry, you will be sleepy. Everything that torments people, that hurts people, that afflicts people—there you will receive each one, you will roll them all together, thus you will suffer there forever. . . .

[Hell is] a very bad place, a great abyss, it stands wide. It is a very frightening place, it is filled with fire, it is very dark, a very gloomy place where the darkness can be held, can be touched. And it stinks so much, it is such a repulsive place; all that stinks of death, that beats one's head lies together there. . . .

And this is what the *tlatlacatecolo* who dwell there are like. Indeed, they are Tzitzimime,[4] they have mouths like Tzitzimime, they have mouths like huts, they have gaping mouths. They have metal bars for teeth, they have curved teeth, they have tongues of flame, their eyes are big burning embers. They have faces on both sides. Their molars are sacrificial stones. Everywhere they eat people, everywhere they bite people, everywhere they gulp people down. They have mouths on all their joints like monsters with which they chew. And they have big long nails. They go about carrying the metal *macuahuitl*[5] of *mictlan*, the metal bar of *mictlan*, the metal wedges of *mictlan* with which they forever beat the wicked. Oh, indeed, like them are they whom you go about following, whom you obey, you, you idolater, you sinner!

---

[2]*mictlan*: Hell.
[3]*tlatlacatecolo*: Shape-shifting demons who brought sickness and death.
[4]*Tzitzimime*: Monster deities of twilight and the end of the world.
[5]*macuahuitl*: Weapons.

7

BERNARDINO DE SAHAGÚN

Christian Psalmody

1583

Singing was an important part of indigenous religious rituals, and Sahagún composed a number of songs and poems with Christian themes to replace existing ones. They circulated in manuscript for many decades, and in 1583 a collection of songs designed for festivals throughout the year was published, the only one of Sahagún's works to be published during his lifetime. In the first three songs included here, Sahagún compares the spiritual "ornaments" offered by Christianity with jade and feathered bracelets, and especially with the flowers that were such an important symbol in Mexica religion. He sets out certain obligations for believers and particularly for men, including nobles. How do the ideals he sets for men differ from those in Mexica culture? In the last four songs, Sahagún compares St. Clare of Assisi (the associate of St. Francis of Assisi who founded a women's religious order similar to Sahagún's male Franciscan order) with Mexica noblewomen. How does he make Clare seem familiar to Mexica hearers? He clearly sees Clare as a model for female converts. What new patterns of behavior does he encourage?

FIRST PSALM

You children, [you] people of New Spain, know, understand that our Lord God has sent you light [and] glory. Honor them; weep for them: for exalted spiritual rank, the spiritual Kingdom are gifts made to you [and] to various people.

Understand [and] realize, you various people, that Christianity, unlike precious green stones, bracelets, emerald-green jade, even rubies smoking like quetzal plumes, is a heavenly thing, a marvelous miracle that the Lord God, that Jesus Himself, came here on earth to give us.

Bernardino de Sahagún's Psalmodia Christiana (Christian Psalmody), translated by Arthur J. O. Anderson (Salt Lake City: University of Utah Press, 1993), 17, 27, 29, 31, 237, 239, 241.

Beloved sons, people of New Spain, realize that your godly goods, your godly shields, your godly insignia [and] ornamentation do exist.

When the sun shone, when day broke, when the Word of God descended upon you, when you received the Sacrament—when you accepted the deep jade-green water of baptism—when God, God the King, adopted you all as His sons, you became spiritual children of the holy Church; your souls acquired godliness [and] in them was placed Christianity, which become your adornment, a gift for you, your lot.

God your Father and your mother holy Church have arranged for you, given you, presented you incomparable feathered bracelets and a variety of precious spiritual flowered vestments: the sign of the cross, and the Creed, and the Lord's Prayer, the Ave Maria, and the Salve Regina. . . .

SECOND PSALM

Spiritual noble lord, great grandee, accept [and] adorn yourself with the precious, incomparable, spiritual turquoise and quetzal-feathered bracelet that your mother holy Church gives you. Five spiritual quetzal feathers are in it, deep green, sharp-pointed, very broad, most wondrous. Nowhere does the like appear.

First, on Sunday and on feast days you are to hear a Mass, and if there is preaching, you are not to leave out, not to omit, the sermon. It is a spiritual torch, a light.

Second, you are to confess when it is Lent and when you go to war or else go to and enter some deadly place, and when you are given one of the Sacraments.

Third, you are to receive the most holy Sacrament, the precious body of our Lord Jesus Christ, when it [is] Easter [and] also when you are seriously sick.

Fourth, you are to fast and abstain from meat in Lent, and during vigils, and . . . on Fridays and Saturdays you are also to do likewise.

Fifth, you are to make offerings; you are to give gifts; you are to dedicate to the church what are called tithes, tenths, and first fruits offerings. All [these] you are to give to the priest; [and] this you are to continue doing each year.

These five commandments of your mother holy Church are the property, the goods, the adornment of Christians. Whoever neglects them, whoever only disdains them, cannot be saved.

You who are a noted, valued Christian, you who are a spiritual noble lord: care for, accept, grasp this; and weep for it, pray for it; and, besides, glory in your spiritual property, your spiritual goods: your due, your lot, your glorification—the quetzal-feathered headband; [your] prodigious glorification—the chaplet of flowers, the plaited necklace, the necklace of radiating pendants, the precious bracelet, the perfect armlet, the precious feathered bracelet.

THIRD PSALM

You who are a Christian, not just anyone; you who are a beloved spiritual son: pay honor to your handful of flowers, your shield of flowers formed of a number of different flowers, the articles that your mother holy Church gives you, which are always to remain held in your hand, in which you will glory: and which you will enjoy [as] you smell them. They are called the virtues, and of these there are seven.

The first is humility, by which pride is destroyed. The second is compassion, by which avarice is destroyed. The third is chastity, by which debauchery is destroyed.

The fourth is patience, by which anger is destroyed. The fifth is moderation, by which gluttony is destroyed. The sixth is love of one's neighbors, by which envy is destroyed. The seventh is diligence, by which laziness is destroyed.

These seven ways of living are those very same precious, very aromatic, very fragrant flowers of all sorts. And the holy Church's beloved sons take great care of them; they pass nights in vigil for them.

Saint Clare, Virgin

SECOND PSALM

Our Lord's hill of flowers lies shining, glowing like the dawn of day. Its concentrated fragrance, its billowing perfume, its odor reaches far.

Red polyanthus, jade green tobacco flowers, red Castilian marigolds, red solandra flowers lovingly burst open; they sparkle, they arch, they sprinkle a golden dew.

Laid out in masses, variegated, rose-hued Castilian marigolds, scarlet feather flowers, [and] golden flowers bend over lovingly and wondrously; they bend over sprinkling a quetzal-colored dew, spreading sunshine, spreading fragrance, a sweet smell.

Above all, at a spring, lives the exquisite, celestial flower, the surpassingly good virgin, Saint Clare, the very awn, the very leading shoot that grows upon God's mountain.

God's beloved Saint Clare, while still a child, opened out her heart to God when she laid down her virginity as a gift before our Lord Jesus Christ.

While still in her father's home, while still a little girl, she paid great heed to fasts and penitence.

THIRD PSALM

"Clara" means brilliant [and] transparent. And in Saint Clare there was indeed true brilliance, which God our Lord had placed in her. She was becoming an example for the women wishing to be chaste.

At this time our beloved Saint Francis lived on earth.

When she heard of the renown of the holy flower custodian, the holy flower gardener, Saint Francis, she followed him; she went to show what was her wish: always to preserve virginity just for God.

And with great joy the holy flower custodian, Saint Francis, heard her words and advised her how to do her tribute work.

He commanded her to set no store by worldly things and to scorn all finery, and to be cloistered in a godly way.

Before an image of the Lady, Saint Mary, he cut off her hair, and she abandoned lordly finery. She put on a habit, a wretched maguey fiber cape. And he gave her what was to be across it, a black cape.

FOURTH PSALM

Then he took Saint Clare as a daughter. She was our beloved father Saint Francis's beloved virgin. Then she cloistered herself. There other virgins gathered.

Now, many virgins, daughters of Saint Clare and of our father, Saint Francis, live together. They are cloistered; they live a spiritual life.

Noblewomen—they esteem good chocolate [and] good food, with flowers, with the "big-ear" spice, with vanilla, pepper, rubber. But Saint Clare drank nothing but pure water.

Folded [tortillas], meat tamales, a strained, fine drink of ground tortillas with chocolate, and its sauce: these are the portion of the noblewomen that they value. But Saint Clare did not taste [these foods]; she had only old tortillas, crumbled ones.

Skirts woven with designs, with the transverse band design, with a design of tawny squared cornerstones, like bed coverlets, are noblewomen's. But as her possessions, Saint Clare had a wretched maguey fiber cape.

Shifts woven with designs, with the quail design; shifts made of coyote fur; rich shifts of all kinds are what noblewomen prize. But God's beloved Saint Clare put on only roughened capes called hair shirts.

FIFTH PSALM

They arrange their hair; they smooth it; it is brushed, washed with soap, wound in braids about the head; they cut [their hair] ends off; they cut it even with the nose; they arrange it to make horns above the forehead. Thus do worldly women deck themselves. But Saint Clare cut off her hair every fifteen days. Just so her daughters do today.

The sinful woman paints her face; she puts dry colored powder on her face; she paints her face yellow, she stains her teeth with cochineal.[1] But God's beloved Saint Clare went with her face covered.

They go about; to and fro along the road they go; they pass among the houses; in the marketplace they pass before one. Women thus cajole one; they wish to be seen. But Saint Clare was only cloistered.

She swept; she washed; she prepared the food. All day she worked. At night God's beloved Saint Clare prayed.

The way of life of God's beloved Saint Clare became like a flower, so fragrant was it the world over. Many virgins followed her way of life.

As our beloved father, Saint Francis, became ruler of the Franciscan Fathers, so also Saint Clare became ruler of the women who are called the godly daughters of Saint Clare.

[1] *cochineal*: Red dye from an insect native to the Americas.

8

ANDRES DE OLMOS

Final Judgment

1530s

Plays as well as songs were written and performed in Nahuatl to convey the Christian message. Religious plays with dramatic action were frequently performed in sixteenth-century Spain in churchyards and marketplaces, and some of these were translated. Other plays were written specifically for a Nahua audience, including this one, which scholars think was written by the Franciscan friar Andres de Olmos, and which was

Barry D. Sell and Louise M. Burkhart, eds., *Nahuatl Theater, Vol. 1: Death and Life in Colonial Nahua Mexico* (Norman: University of Oklahoma Press, 2004), 191, 193, 201, 203, 205, 207, 209.

performed in several places in the 1530s. The play depicts the Last Judgment, the point in Christian understandings of the end of the world at which Christ will judge each person. Characters include allegorical figures such as Penance, Church, Time, and Death that were common in European religious plays, and also the allegorical figure Sweeping, who calls sinners to reform. As we saw in the chapter introduction, sweeping altars and temples was a devotional activity in Mexica religion, as dirt was linked to cosmic disorder. How is sweeping made into a Christian activity in this play? The play centers on the fate of Lucía, a Nahua woman who did not marry in a Christian ceremony. Catholic doctrine held that marriage was one of seven sacraments, rituals that mediate grace between God and the recipient. How does this doctrine determine the fate of Lucía here?

(Wind instruments are played. Heaven opens. Saint Michael descends.)

SAINT MICHAEL: O creations of God! Know, and indeed you already know, for it is in the sacred commands of our lord God, that he will finish off, he will destroy the world that his precious and honored father, God, made. He will destroy, he will finish off all that he made, the various birds, the various living creatures, along with you. He will destroy you, you people of the world. But be certain that the dead will revive. The good and proper ones who served the just judge, the sentencer, God, he will take to his royal home, the place of eternal and utter bliss, glory, the place of utter bliss of all the male and female saints. But the bad ones who did not serve our lord God, may they be certain that they will merit suffering in the place of the dead. So then, weep, remember it. Fear it, be scared to death, for the day of judgment will happen to you. It is very frightening, it is very shocking, it scares people to death, it makes people faint with fright. So then, emend your lives. The day of judgment is about to happen to you. It is the time, it is the moment, now.

(Wind instruments are played. Saint Michael ascends. Penance enters [along with] Time, Holy Church, Sweeping, [and] Death.)...

HOLY CHURCH: I am the compassionate mother of the one who appointed me, my precious son Jesus Christ, so that here on account of the people of earth I am always weeping, especially when one of them dies. Therefore I spill my tears. I beseech my precious mother, sacred fountain of utter happiness, to have compassion for them, to illuminate his creatures. . . . I will feed them,

I will give them drink if they are thirsty. And now I am waiting for them. I am sad for their sakes. May they come, and may they come to emend their lives, may they pray. They will receive compassion. And may they weep and be sad because of their sins, their defects. SWEEPING: You are his mother of perfect and complete faith. It is all correct, what you say. They do not remember what they do not desire; they just want to go on sinning. Do I not exert all my effort? I always cry out to them, every day. I induce them to sweep things, to keep vigil, to arise in the morning, to do penance, to suffer cold, that is, in a sacred way to sweep their spirits, their souls, to fast, to abstain from food so that they will receive compassion and be pardoned. And if not, there is no way at all that they will be able to enter the royal home of our lord God....

(Heaven opens. Christ enters. He leads forth Saint Michael, who brings scales. And Christ brings forth a cross. He stands at the edge of heaven. And the Antichrist rushes in. Things explode.)

CHRIST: Come, my war leader, Saint Michael. Here in heaven it is now high time that I bring time to an end, that I destroy it. It is called Final Judgment, the day of judging people. As I set down in my sacred commands, I will sweep things, I will purify heaven and earth. The people of earth, the living and the dead, have greatly dirtied things because of their bad lives. And now, awaken them, the living and the dead, the good and the bad. And to the good ones I will give their heavenly flowery riches, heavenly jades and garments, heavenly palm fronds. But as for the bad, may they be certain that the house of the place of the dead and the sufferings of the place of the dead will become their possessions, because they were not able to keep my sacred commands.

(Christ descends; [also] Saint Michael. Christ sits down.)

CHRIST: I have already given you orders as to what you will do, my war leader.
SAINT MICHAEL: Very well, O my beloved teacher. Let the dead come to life, let the living rouse themselves. Let them take their bones and collect them, and let them take on their earth, their clay. Give them reviving, [through] the Holy Spirit, along with their souls, so that they will be able to answer you, so that they will say what they did that was good and what they did that was bad, their deeds....

(Saint Michael plays a wind instrument. Then they each go before Christ. He sits down. [Dead and living persons enter.] And the angel weighs things on a scale. First Dead Person kneels.)

CHRIST: Come, you! Did you carry out my commands while you were still living on earth, you were flitting about? Speak. Answer me, the way that you used to speak on earth. Speak in the same way now.

FIRST DEAD PERSON: O my deity, O my ruler, I carried out, I worked at, I fulfilled your sacred commands. I carried out your orders. Ask my [guardian] angel, O my beloved teacher.

CHRIST: Thank you. In heaven you will be utterly happy, you will prosper. Your joyfulness will never be finished or come to an end.

(He blesses him. Saint Michael pushes him to Christ's right-hand side.)

CHRIST: Come, you living one. Whom did you honor on earth, and whom did you love?

FIRST LIVING PERSON: You, you who are my deity, you who are my ruler.

CHRIST: If it is true that I am your deity, I am your ruler, did you carry out my sacred commands? Did you fulfill them?

FIRST LIVING PERSON: I did not do it, O my deity. Pardon me. I am a sinner.

CHRIST: Today there no longer is any pardon at all. Go!

(Saint Michael pushes [First] Living Person to the other side. Then Second Dead Person kneels before Christ.)

CHRIST: Come, you who were dead. What did you do while you still lived on earth? Did you work for me? Did you serve me on earth? Answer me!

SECOND DEAD PERSON: Not at all. Pardon me, O my ruler, O my teacher, O God!

CHRIST: Today in the time of judgment there is no longer any pardon. Go!

(Saint Michael pushes [Second] Dead Person away. And the demons drag him off. They lay him on the other side. Second Living Person, Lucía, kneels.) . . .

CHRIST: Come, you who are a living person! Did you carry out my sacred commands, the ten of them? Did you love your neighbors, and your father and your mother?

SECOND LIVING PERSON, LUCÍA: Yes. It is you, my deity, my ruler, whom I loved first, afterwards my father and my mother.

CHRIST: If it is true that I am your deity and you loved me first and afterward your father and your mother, did you carry out my commands, and the command of my beloved honored mother, in the seventh sacrament, marrying in a sacred way? Did you guard yourself in a sacred way when you lived on earth? What have you accomplished?

LUCÍA: No. I did not work for you and I did not recognize your beloved mother. Pardon me, O my deity, O my ruler!

CHRIST: Now, truly your heart never spoke to us on earth. It was only your lustful living that you used to work at. Go, do it. Perhaps you are forgetting something else of your lustful living. Work at it. Be certain that you may hope for nothing in heaven. How unfortunate you are now, that you never wanted to get married on earth. You have won the house of the place of the dead. You have merited it. Go! See those whom you served. I do not know you.

(He pushes her toward the demons.) . . .

LUCÍA: Ah! Ah! How unfortunate I am! I am a sinner. I have merited suffering in the place of the dead. If only I had not been born on earth! Ah! Ah! May the earth be entirely cursed, and the time in which I was born. May my mother who made me also be despised! Ah! May the breast milk with which I was nurtured be despised! May that which I used to eat and that which I used to drink on earth be despised. Ah! May the earth I used to kick be despised, and the rags I used to wear, for they all have turned into fire! Ah! Greatly do they burn me, the fire butterflies that come hanging here from my ears. They signify how I used to beautify myself with my earrings. And here, wound around my neck, is a very frightening fire serpent. It signifies my necklaces that I used to put on. And here I come girded with a very frightening fire serpent, the heart of the house of the place of the dead. It signifies how I used to enjoy myself on earth. Ah! Ah! If only I had gotten married! Ah! How unfortunate I am!

FIRST DEMON: Now you will pay a penalty, you will make restitution for everything. You had no esteem for your neighbors on earth.

(They beat her.)

SATAN: Get moving, O wicked one! Not until now do you remember that you should have gotten married? How is it that you did not remember it while you were still living on earth? But now you will make restitution for all your wickedness. Run along! Get moving!

(They beat her. Just thus they make her go in. Things explode. The demons play wind instruments. Then Priest enters.)

PRIEST: O my beloved children, O Christians, O creations of God! Now you have seen an ominous marvel! It is correct. It is written in the sacred book. Be prudent! Rouse yourselves, look at yourselves in the mirror, the way that it happened to your neighbor. And may it not happen to you the same way. It is a model, a measuring stick, which our lord God gives us. Tomorrow or the next day, the day of judgment is going to happen. Just pray to our lord, Jesus Christ, and to the noblewoman, Saint Mary, that she pray to her beloved honored child, Jesus Christ, so that afterward you will merit and obtain joyfulness in heaven, glory. May it so be done.

Ave Maria.

9

CHIMALPAHIN

Annals

1613

It is easier to find information about how Christian ideas were communicated in New Spain than about how people responded, as most of the surviving sources come from the pens of Spanish clergy and officials. One exception are the annals of the indigenous chronicler Chimalpahin, who was introduced in Document 5. Chimalpahin was a Christian and a church official, and in the annals covering his own lifetime he includes descriptions of many religious activities in which Spanish, native, African, and mestizo people participated. One of the most common of these were church processions in honor of Jesus, Mary, or one of the saints, such as those held during the week before Easter, which is described here. Confraternities of laypeople, often dedicated to one individual or a particular

Don Domingo Francisco de San Antón Muñon Chimalpahin Quauhtlehuanitzin, *Annals of His Time*, edited and translated by James Lockhart, Susan Schroeder, and Doris Namala (Stanford, Calif.: Stanford University Press, 2006), 241, 243, 245, 247.

element of Christian religious practice, marched in these processions in groups. How did people express their religious devotion in these processions?

Today, Monday of Holy Week, the 1st day of the month of April of the year 1613, in the afternoon, was when for the second time there marched in procession the people of Santa María Cuepopan, the members who belong to the cofradía[1] of the Souls [of Purgatory], that father fray Diego Mejía established there for their help. With his cord girdle, his rope belt, our precious father San Francisco[2] helps them and extracts them from the place where people are purified by fire, purgatory, for so he appeared going along; when they went in procession they carried [an image of] San Francisco on a carrying platform freeing the souls with his said cord girdle, his rope, from the said purgatory by order of our lord God, and other things from his Passion [were in evidence]. The procession was in the afternoon; they started from their church and passed by the nuns of Concepción at Ayoticpac; next they came by the nuns of the Visitación; next they came by the church of San Francisco; next they came by the Casa Profesa of San Ignacio; then they came by the cathedral. . . .

Today, the third day, Holy Wednesday, in the afternoon, was when the miscellaneously assembled people from Michoacan[3] and some Mexica went in procession for the first time; they established their new cofradía at the royal hospital of Nuestra Señora de la Caridad, where we commoners are treated; the cofradía is dedicated to our said precious mother. A second cofradía there is dedicated to San Nicolás de Tolentino; from it only a few more came along in the procession. They went in procession over a long route coming as far as the cathedral. —

Likewise the same said Holy Wednesday in the afternoon was when the cofradía members from Santiago Tlatelolco who are dedicated to the death of our precious father San Francisco came out in procession; they too came out in great splendor, they too went shooting off many rockets, again they came as far as the cathedral; they went in procession over the entire same route. . . .

Today, the fifth day, Good Friday, at 1 o'clock in the morning, while it was still full nighttime, the people of Santa Cruz Contzinco came out

---

[1] *cofradía*: Confraternity.
[2] *San Francisco*: Saint Francis of Assisi.
[3] *Michoacan*: Indigenous people from outside Mexico City.

and went in procession for the first time with [an image of] the burial of our lord God. . . .

And also on the said Good Friday, in the afternoon, there was a procession for the burial of the death of our lord God from Santiago Tlatelolco; today was the first time that the Tlatelolca brought [the image] all the way to the cathedral in procession, as they had never done each year previously. It was very marvelous how the whole passion of our lord God went lined up. This brought to an end all the processions that have passed by here.

2

Europe: Reforms and
Reformations in Christianity

BACKGROUND

At the same time that Europeans were establishing colonial empires
and attempting to convert indigenous populations to Christianity,
Christianity in western Europe splintered. This split was rooted in the
role of the church as a political and economic institution, as well as its
religious doctrines and practices. In 1450 the church in central and
western Europe was a hierarchy headed by the pope, who claimed
spiritual authority over all Christians as well as political authority over
the inhabitants of the papal states. Papal authority rested in theory on
statements in the New Testament that were understood to give special
powers to the apostle Peter, who was regarded as the first pope. In
practice papal authority also rested on a strong centralized bureau-
cracy. The church owned about one-quarter of the land in Europe, and
higher officials, including bishops and the pope, often came from
noble families and lived lavishly. Each diocese—the territory administered by a bishop—was divided into parishes, which were to be
staffed by parish priests.

Along with parishes and dioceses, the western Christian church
also maintained thousands of monasteries and convents, where individuals lived communally under the leadership of an abbot or abbess.
Monks and nuns took special vows of poverty, chastity, and obedience,
and lived according to a monastic rule, which regulated the pattern of
work, prayer, and other devotional activities during each day. Individual monks and nuns did not own any property, but monasteries and
convents often held large territories and governed villages and peasants. Friars, such as the Dominicans and the Franciscans, were similar
to monks and nuns in that they took special vows, but they lived out in
the world rather than in cloistered houses, traveling from town to
town preaching, ministering to the poor, or teaching at a university.

Almost all Europeans were officially Christian and paid taxes directly to the church. They were taught, and most believed, that the guidance of priests and the rituals of the church were necessary for salvation. People often made donations to monasteries and convents, in return for which priests, monks, and nuns said prayers for the soul of the donor or a beloved family member, designed to speed the path to heaven. People also did a number of things themselves to help achieve salvation or ask God's blessing. They learned from their priests that good works as well as faith were necessary to get into heaven, so they attended church, gave money for the poor, prayed before eating and sleeping, and went on pilgrimages to holy places. People participated in processions dedicated to the Virgin Mary or a specific saint. They confessed their sins to the village priest, who then set certain actions, such as praying or fasting, as penance for those sins. Such penance might be lessened or eliminated through the granting of indulgences, which were certificates issued by the church that remitted the earthly punishments owed to God because of sin.

The Roman Catholic Church was a powerful institution, and religious devotion was a central aspect of people's lives, but there was also dissatisfaction, which had been growing since the twelfth century. People complained that bishops did not live in their dioceses and did not supervise priests very well; that monks and friars were greedy and immoral, wheedling money out of people, maintaining concubines, and living too well; that priests just mumbled the mass in Latin without understanding what the words meant. Many thought the pope and bishops had too much power and that they gained money by leading people to believe that donations alone, without faith, would get them into heaven.

Calls for reform became louder in the early sixteenth century, especially among Christian humanists, such as Desiderius Erasmus and Juan Luis Vives (1492–1540), who regarded humanist learning as a way to bring about reform of the church and a deepening of people's spiritual lives. In both serious works and in satires, Erasmus accused the church of greed, corruption, and desire for power. He advocated better education for both clergy and laity, hoping that people might be convinced to spend their time on prayer instead of pilgrimages, and their money on helping the needy instead of buying indulgences. (See Document 10.)

In the second decade of the sixteenth century, Martin Luther, an Augustinian friar and professor of theology at Wittenberg University in Germany, joined the chorus calling for reform. Luther was greatly troubled by doubts about his own worth and sinfulness, and in reflection on the Bible found the basis of an understanding of essential Christian doctrines different from the one he had been taught. His understanding is often codified as "by faith alone, by grace alone, by Scripture alone" (*sola fide, sola gratia, sola Scriptura*). For Christians, according to Luther, salvation and justification come through faith, not good works, although true faith leads to love and to the active expression of faith in helping others. Faith is a gift of God, not the result of human effort. God's word is revealed only in scripture (that is, the Bible), not in the traditions of the church. (See Document 11.)

Luther, and soon many others, argued that the pope's supreme authority in the church was not based on the Bible, that the church should give up much of its wealth, and that the prayers of priests or monks were no more powerful than those of ordinary Christians. They thought that religious services and the Bible should be in the languages people spoke, instead of Latin, which was restricted to a learned elite. They believed that no one should take special vows or live in monasteries, but that men and women should get married and live in families, serving God through their work or family life. (See Document 12.) People should go to church and pray, but pray directly to God or Jesus, not to the Virgin Mary or the saints, who might have been good people but had no special powers or claim to holiness.

Most Christian humanists such as Erasmus wanted reforms within the existing church structure. By the early 1520s, however, some reformers, including Luther, advocated a break from Rome. He and his followers called their movement "evangelical," from the Greek word *euangelion*[1] meaning "gospel" or "good news." Later the movement that Luther started came to be known as the Protestant Reformation after a 1529 document issued by German princes protesting an order that they give up their religious innovations.

The Protestant reformers published their criticisms and ideas using the new technology of the printing press, and many people found them appealing. (See Document 13.) City dwellers supported the idea that the church should not have special privileges, and in the countryside, peasants liked the emphasis on the Bible and the idea that the clergy were no better than anyone else. Protestant ideas were attractive to political leaders, who broke with the papacy and the Roman church and established their own churches, with bishops and priests who received a salary from the state. Through a complex process that

[1] eh-ven-GHEL-ee-on.

involved intellectual debate, preaching, political decisions, and war, by the middle of the sixteenth century, most of central and northern Europe had split from the Catholic Church.

In the 1520s and early 1530s, the Catholic Church reacted rather fitfully to humanist and Protestant challenges, but beginning with Pope Paul III (pontificate 1534–1549), the papal court became the center of the reform movement within the Catholic Church, later called the Catholic Reformation. Paul appointed reform-minded cardinals, abbots, and bishops who improved education for the clergy, tried to enforce moral standards among them, and worked on correcting the most glaring abuses. Paul III and his successors supported the establishment of new religious orders that preached to the common people, the opening of seminaries for the training of priests, and stricter control of clerical life. Their own lives were models of decorum and piety, in contrast to the fifteenth- and early-sixteenth-century popes who had concentrated on decorating churches and palaces and on enhancing the power of their own families. By 1600 the papacy had been reestablished as a spiritual force in Europe, with its political hold on central Italy suffering no decline in the process.

Paul III also took a stance in the developing debate about the peoples of the New World. Theologians and legal scholars debated whether any European ruler had the right to claim ownership of lands in the New World. Were the peoples of the New World like children, who had no right to reject conversion or to hold their own land, or did they have the same rights as Europeans? In the papal bull *Sublimus Dei*, promulgated in 1537, Paul declared that the indigenous people of the Americas were rational beings with souls and thus should not be enslaved. *Sublimus Dei* was subsequently used by those who advocated more humane treatment of native peoples by Spanish settlers, though it was difficult to enforce at a distance, and brutal treatment of indigenous peoples continued. Many missionaries agreed with its central assertion, however, and the materials they produced to win converts approached them as sophisticated hearers, rather than childlike and naive. (See Documents 7 and 8.)

Reforming popes also sought to combat the spread of Protestant teaching. In fact, many historians view the Catholic Reformation as two interrelated movements, one a drive for internal reform linked to earlier reform efforts, and the other a counter-Reformation that opposed Protestants intellectually, institutionally, politically, and militarily. Paul III initiated the Roman Inquisition, which investigated those suspected of heresy. In the 1550s popes promulgated an Index of Prohibited Books, which forbade the printing, distribution, and reading of books and authors judged heretical.

Reforms involved religious orders as well as the papacy. Older religious orders carried out measures to restore discipline and get back to their original aims, and new religious orders were founded with a variety of aims. The most important of the new religious orders was the Society of Jesus, or the Jesuits, founded by Ignatius Loyola in 1534. Loyola was a Spanish nobleman who read books about saints and martyrs while healing from horrendously painful battle injuries. He decided to give up his life as a soldier and instead devote himself to the pope and the Catholic Church. Loyola's charismatic personality and tremendous energy attracted other dedicated young men, and in 1540 he and his followers gained papal approval for the Jesuits to carry out action on behalf of the Catholic Church. Admission into the Jesuit order took many years, during which time the young man went through intensive training designed to transform him into a spiritual soldier controlled from within. (See Document 14.)

The Jesuits' main callings were to educate and convert, so they founded schools, taught at universities, and preached popular sermons. They became confessors to influential people, and through this gained influence at many European courts. In Europe, they became very effective at stopping the further spread of Protestant ideas, and even reconverted some areas to Catholicism. Jesuit missionaries traveled to places far beyond Europe, including New Spain, Brazil, India, China, and Japan.

The achievements of the Jesuits made many women eager to found a similar organization for women, but church leaders were horrified at the idea of women out in public preaching and teaching. Popes refused to grant approval for an order of religious women with an active mission in the world. Instead they encouraged women to pray for Catholic successes, from their homes if they were married and from behind the walls of their convents if they were nuns. Teresa of Avila, a Spanish nun, chose to see this encouragement as a call to action. A mystic motivated by intense visions of Christ and the angels, Teresa traveled around Spain from the 1560s to the 1580s, establishing new convents and reforming existing ones to bring them back to stricter standards of asceticism and poverty. Although some Catholic officials opposed her actions as improper for a woman, she saw them as a defense of her faith against Protestant challenges. (See Document 15.) Teresa's ideas and actions were later approved by the Catholic Church; both she and Ignatius Loyola were canonized as saints in

1622. Other Catholic women were bolder, setting up convents in places where European countries were establishing colonies.

An affirmation of the necessity of cloistering for all women religious was just one of many decrees issued by the Council of Trent, an ecumenical council convened by Pope Paul III in 1545, which met intermittently over the next eighteen years to define Catholic doctrine and reform abuses. Trent issued many decrees stipulating reforms and reasserting traditional Catholic beliefs in response to both humanists and Protestants. (See Document 16.) Although Trent's ideals would be realized only slowly, by the time the council finally disbanded, the Catholic Church had clearly begun to change. The church had revived traditional doctrine, provided the means for the enforcement of theological uniformity through such measures as the Papal Index, and begun to reform itself through the new religious orders with their emphasis on discipline and education.

This revitalization did not simply affect the church hierarchy, but also devotional life at the local level. As in the Spanish colonies of the New World, confraternities of lay people were established or expanded in many urban parishes and even in villages; they held processions and feasts, handed out charity to the poor, purchased furnishings and art for churches, administered hospitals and orphanages, engaged in penitential flagellation, and supported local shrines and altars. By the end of the sixteenth century, this reinvigorated Catholic Church had been successful in halting Protestant advances in Europe, and had taken Catholicism around the world.

The second half of the sixteenth century also saw further developments in the Protestant Reformation, with the most dynamic form of Protestantism inspired by John Calvin (1509–1564). Calvin was born in France and originally studied law; in about 1533 he became a Protestant and fled to Switzerland, where several years later he published the *Institutes of the Christian Religion*, a synthesis of Protestant thought arranged in a logical, systematic way. In the *Institutes*, Calvin sets out his key doctrines: God is infinite in power and sovereignty; humans are completely sinful and depraved, saved only through the atoning power of Jesus Christ; redemptive grace and the possibility of union with Christ are gifts of God; God determined who would be saved through the redemptive power of Christ and who would not, a choice not based on any human actions. (See Document 17.) The latter idea, called *predestination* or *election*, had been asserted by Christian thinkers since St. Augustine in the fourth century and discussed even earlier, but Calvin made it absolute.

One's own behavior could do nothing to change one's fate, but many Calvinists came to believe that hard work, thrift, and proper moral conduct could serve as signs that one was among the "elect" chosen for salvation. Salvation had already been decided, so that human energies could be put to fulfilling God's will in the world, which could be done through diligence, thanksgiving, and dedication in one's personal life and work. Calvinism appealed to a wide spectrum of people, but its vigor and dynamism proved especially popular with urban merchants, professionals, and artisans. Calvin put his ideas into action in the Swiss city of Geneva, which he transformed into a community based on his religious principles. (See Document 18.)

Calvinism soon became an ideology with potentially revolutionary political implications. Calvin's ideas spread in the mid-sixteenth century into France, the Netherlands, Germany, England, Scotland, Hungary, and Poland. Outside Geneva Calvinists established regional representative institutions to make decisions about broader issues of church policy. In all bodies, from local congregations to regional institutions, laymen worked with clergy to set church policy. This was different from Lutheran churches, which had generally retained a hierarchy of bishops and in which the territorial ruler was the only layperson with much power. Calvinist pastors did have great influence, but the fact that laymen had a strong voice in running the church—a more democraticized form of church government—was something new. This enhanced the appeal of Calvinism for many groups, and offered some a platform for political grievances. Nobles in France and urban residents in the Netherlands found in Calvinism a way to combat the power of the monarchy as well as the papacy, and the later sixteenth century saw religious wars in many parts of Europe, as a reinvigorated Catholicism met a more militant Protestantism.

DOCUMENTS

There are a huge number of sources available for studying reforms in early modern western Christianity. The most important humanist and Protestant reformers were highly learned men who wrote extensively, and their works were quickly printed on the new printing press with movable metal type. The market for religious works of all types was very strong, and the writings of reformers sold especially well, in particular those that expressed widely held criticism of the church in lively language or vicious invective. Perhaps as many as one-fourth of the works printed in Germany in the sixteenth century were written by Martin Luther, including sermons, lectures, and pamphlets. John Calvin's writings were fewer, but their global impact was greater. The official churches of the Netherlands and Scotland were set up on Calvinist models, English and American Puritans adopted Calvinist notions of godly discipline, and Calvinist theories about the right to resist tyrannical rulers influenced later revolutionaries in Europe and the Americas.

Works by Catholic authors sold less widely in the first half of the sixteenth century than did those by Protestants, in part because defenses of tradition are rarely as much fun to read as attacks, and in part because Church leaders did not support publishing religious works in vernacular languages. By the later sixteenth century, however, more Catholic works were available, including polemics against Protestants, sermons, stories of the saints, guides to prayer, and official statements of faith.

As you examine these documents, you can identify and compare the way the main themes emerge in them. Erasmus (Document 10), Luther (Document 11), and the artist Matthias Gerung (Document 13) all criticize papal power and the Catholic hierarchy; how is this criticism answered by Ignatius Loyola (Document 14) and Pius IV (Document 16)? How would you compare ideas about God's authority and the power of the human will in Loyola (Document 14) with those of Calvin (Document 17)? Luther (Document 12) and Loyola (Document 14) both set out ideals for proper behavior among Christian men; how do their ideals of masculinity differ, and how are they the same? How would you compare the ideal set out for women in Luther (Document 12) and Teresa of Avila (Document 15)? (For questions that relate these sources to those in other chapters in the book, see p. 163.)

10

DESIDERIUS ERASMUS

The Praise of Folly

1511

Desiderius Erasmus[1] was the most famous scholar of his time in all of Europe. He published a new Latin translation of the New Testament alongside the first printed Greek text in 1516, a six-volume edition of the works of St. Jerome, and many other scholarly works on biblical texts. Erasmus also wrote a number of works that became popular with the growing number of middle-class readers. In his scholarly and his popular writings, and in the hundreds of letters he sent to scholars, friends, rulers, and admirers around Europe, Erasmus criticized the church and called for a renewal of the ideals of the early church. This renewal would be based on what Erasmus termed his "philosophy of Christ," which emphasized inner spirituality and personal morality rather than scholastic theology or outward observances of piety such as pilgrimages. Despite his harsh criticism, Erasmus never broke with the Catholic Church and in the 1520s engaged in a bitter literary debate with Luther about human free will. Erasmus's most popular work was The Praise of Folly, *a witty satire poking fun at political, social, and especially religious institutions, which went through many editions in his lifetime in a number of languages. Folly is a demi-goddess—like Justice—and the main text is her speech arguing that everything in life comes from her. What does Erasmus—speaking in Folly's voice—criticize about monks and the pope here? How does Folly compare the lives of the current pope with those of Christ and early Christian leaders?*

[Then there] are the men who generally call themselves "the religious" and "monks"[2]—utterly false names both, since most of them keep as far away as they can from religion and no people are more in evidence in every sort of place. But I do not see how anything could

[1]deh-seh-DEHR-ee-us eh-RAS-mus.
[2]The word *monk* comes from the Latin word for "alone."

Desiderius Erasmus, *The Praise of Folly*, translated by Hoyt Hopewell Hudson (Princeton, N.J.: Princeton University Press, 1941), 85–86, 98–100.

be more dismal than these monks if I did not succor them in many ways. For though people as a whole so detest this race of men that meeting one by accident is supposed to be bad luck, yet they flatter themselves to the queen's taste. For one thing, they reckon it the highest degree of piety to have no contact with literature, and hence they see to it that they do not know how to read. For another, when with asinine voices they bray out in church those psalms they have learned, by rote rather than by heart, they are convinced that they are anointing God's ears with the blandest of oil. Some of them make a good profit from their dirtiness and mendicancy, collecting their food from door to door with importunate bellowing; nay, there is not an inn, public conveyance, or ship where they do not intrude, to the great disadvantage of the other common beggars. Yet according to their account, by their very dirtiness, ignorance, want of manners, and insolence, these delightful fellows are representing to us the lives of the apostles. . . .

As to these Supreme Pontiffs who take the place of Christ, . . . as it is now, what labor turns up to be done they hand over to Peter and Paul,[3] who have leisure for it. But the splendor and the pleasure they take care of personally. And so it comes about—by my doing, remember—that scarcely any kind of men live more softly or less oppressed with care; believing that they are amply acceptable to Christ if with a mystical and almost theatrical finery, with ceremonies, and with those titles of Beatitude and Reverence and Holiness, along with blessing and cursing, they perform the office of bishops. To work miracles is primitive and old-fashioned, hardly suited to our times; to instruct the people is irksome; to interpret the Holy Scriptures is pedantry; to pray is otiose; to shed tears is distressing and womanish; to live in poverty is sordid; to be beaten in war is dishonorable and less than worthy of one who will hardly admit kings, however great, to kiss his sacred foot; and finally, to die is unpleasant, to die on the cross a disgrace.

There remain only those weapons and sweet benedictions of which Paul speaks, and the popes are generous enough with these: interdictions, excommunications, reexcommunications, anathematizations, pictured damnations, and the terrific lightning-bolt of the bull, which by its mere flicker sinks the souls of men below the floor of hell. And these most holy fathers in Christ, and vicars of Christ, launch it against no one with more spirit than against those who, at the instigation of the devil, try to impair or to subtract from the patrimony of

---

[3] *Peter and Paul*: Two apostles in the New Testament.

Peter.[4] Although this saying of Peter's stands in the Gospel, "We have left all and followed Thee," yet they give the name of his patrimony to lands, towns, tribute, imposts, and moneys. On behalf of these things, inflamed by zeal for Christ, they fight with fire and sword, not without shedding of Christian blood; and then they believe they have defended the bride of Christ[5] in apostolic fashion, having scattered what they are pleased to designate as "her enemies." As if the church had any enemies more pestilential than impious pontiffs who by their silence allow Christ to be forgotten, who enchain Him by mercenary rules, adulterate His teaching by forced interpretations, and crucify Him afresh by their scandalous life!

[4]*patrimony of Peter*: The property belonging to the papacy.
[5]*bride of Christ*: The Roman Catholic Church.

11

MARTIN LUTHER

The Freedom of a Christian

1520

In 1517, Luther began preaching and writing against indulgences. He was ordered to come to Rome, but the unstable and complicated political situation in Germany allowed him to avoid this. He refused to take back his ideas and moved further and further away from Catholic theology. In 1520 he published three pamphlets that mark his clear break with the papacy: Address to the Christian Nobility of the German Nation, *demanding that German rulers reform the church;* The Babylonian Captivity of the Church, *condemning the papacy for holding Christians in "captivity" for centuries by distorting the meaning of the sacraments;* The Freedom of a Christian *(sometimes translated as* On Christian Liberty*), summarizing his own beliefs. The pope responded by excommunicating Luther. How does Luther here describe human nature and the power of God? What is the believer to do in order to achieve salvation?*

Luther's Works, ed. Harold Grimm (Philadelphia: Muhlenberg Press, 1957), 31:345, 346, 348, 359.

Man has a twofold nature, a spiritual and a bodily one. According to the spiritual nature, which men refer to as the soul, he is called a spiritual, inner, or new man. According to the bodily nature, which men refer to as flesh, he is called a carnal, outward, or old man, of whom the Apostle writes in II Cor. 4 [:16], "Though our outer nature is wasting away, our inner nature is being renewed every day." Because of this diversity of nature the Scriptures assert contradictory things concerning the same man, since these two men in the same man contradict each other, "for the desires of the flesh are against the Spirit, and the desires of the Spirit are against the flesh," according to Gal. 5 [:17].

First, let us consider the inner man to see how a righteous, free, and pious Christian, that is, a spiritual, new, and inner man, becomes what he is. It is evident that no external thing has any influence in producing Christian righteousness or freedom, or in producing unrighteousness or servitude. A simple argument will furnish the proof of this statement. What can it profit the soul if the body is well, free, and active, and eats, drinks, and does as it pleases? For in these respects even the most godless slaves of vice may prosper. On the other hand, how will poor health or imprisonment or hunger or thirst or any other external misfortune harm the soul? Even the most godly men, and those who are free because of clear consciences, are afflicted with these things. None of these things touch either the freedom or the servitude of the soul. It does not help the soul if the body is adorned with the sacred robes of priests or dwells in sacred places or is occupied with sacred duties or prays, fasts, abstains from certain kinds of food, or does any work that can be done by the body and in the body. The righteousness and the freedom of the soul require something far different since the things which have been mentioned could be done by any wicked person. Such works produce nothing but hypocrites. . . .

One thing, and only one thing, is necessary for Christian life, righteousness, and freedom. That one thing is the most holy Word of God, the gospel of Christ, as Christ says, John 11 [:25], "I am the resurrection and the life; he who believes in me, though he die, yet shall he live"; and John 8 [:36], "So if the Son makes you free, you will be free indeed"; and Matt. 4 [:4], "Man shall not live by bread alone, but by every word that proceeds from the mouth of God." . . .

Let this suffice concerning the inner man, his liberty, and the source of his liberty, the righteousness of faith. He needs neither laws nor good works but, on the contrary, is injured by them if he believes that he is justified by them.

Now let us turn to the second part, the outer man. Here we shall answer all those who, offended by the word "faith" and by all that has been said, now ask, "If faith does all things and is alone sufficient unto righteousness, why then are good works commanded? We will take our ease and do no works and be content with faith." I answer: not so, you wicked men, not so. That would indeed be proper if we were wholly inner and perfectly spiritual men. But such we shall be only at the last day, the day of the resurrection of the dead. As long as we live in the flesh we only begin to make some progress in that which shall be perfected in the future life. . . .

Although, as I have said, a man is abundantly and sufficiently justified by faith inwardly, in his spirit, and so has all that he needs, except insofar as this faith and these riches must grow from day to day even to the future life; yet he remains in this mortal life on earth. In this life he must control his own body and have dealings with men. Here the works begin; here a man cannot enjoy leisure; here he must indeed take care to discipline his body by fastings, watchings, labors, and other reasonable discipline and to subject it to the Spirit so that it will obey and conform to the inner man and faith and not revolt against faith and hinder the inner man, as it is the nature of the body to do if it is not held in check. The inner man, who by faith is created in the image of God, is both joyful and happy because of Christ in whom so many benefits are conferred upon him; and therefore it is his one occupation to serve God joyfully and without thought of gain, in love that is not constrained.

While he is doing this, behold, he meets a contrary will in his own flesh which strives to serve the world and seeks its own advantage. This the spirit of faith cannot tolerate, but with joyful zeal it attempts to put the body under control and hold it in check. . . .

In doing these works, however, we must not think that a man is justified before God by them, for faith, which alone is righteousness before God, cannot endure that erroneous opinion. We must, however, realize that these works reduce the body to subjection and purify it of its evil lusts, and our whole purpose is to be directed only toward the driving out of lusts. Since by faith the soul is cleansed and made to love God, it desires that all things, and especially its own body, shall be purified so that all things may join with it in loving and praising God. Hence a man cannot be idle, for the need of his body drives him and he is compelled to do many good works to reduce it to subjection. Nevertheless the works themselves do not justify him before God, but he does the works out of spontaneous love in obedience to God.

12

MARTIN LUTHER

A Sermon on Marriage

1525

Among the many Catholic teachings that Luther rejected was the notion that virginity was superior to marriage and that life in a convent or monastery, which generally involved taking a vow of celibacy, was better than family life. One of his earliest treatises attacked vows of celibacy and argued that the best Christian life is one in which sexual activity is channeled into marriage; he returned to this theme again and again. Luther was adamant that marriage was not a sacrament, as it was held to be in Catholic theology, for it conferred no special grace, but it was the ideal state for almost everyone. This is a section of one of Luther's many sermons on marriage; six months after he preached this, he followed his own advice and married a former nun, Katharina von Bora. The marriage produced six children. How does he describe here the obligations of the wife and husband toward each other? In what way are these religious duties?

God has laid a serious command upon marriage, just like a gardener who, having a lovely herb or rose garden that he loves and does not want anyone to climb in and break anything off or do damage to it, builds a fence around it. God does just this with the Sixth Commandment: "You shall not commit adultery." For marriage is His most beloved herb or rose garden, in which the most beautiful little roses

Luther on Women: A Sourcebook, edited and translated by Susan C. Karant-Nunn and Merry E. Wiesner-Hanks (Cambridge: Cambridge University Press, 2003), 94–95.

and carnations grow, and these are the dear children of humans, who are created in the image of God. They come out and are born so that the human race is maintained. So God bids one to keep marriage in the fear of God, in modesty and honor, and not to commit adultery. For whoever commits adultery God will punish horribly in body and soul and cast out of His kingdom. . . .

Men should govern their wives not with great cudgels, flails, or drawn knives, but rather with friendly words and gestures and with all gentleness so that they do not become shy . . . and take fright such that they afterward do not know what to do. Thus, men should rule their wives with reason and not unreason, and honor the feminine sex as the weakest vessel and also as coheirs of the grace of life. . . .

"Women, be subject to your husbands as to the Lord, for the husband is the head of the wife" [Eph. 5:22–23]. Again to the Colossians in the third chapter [3:18]. Because of this, the wife has not been created out of the head, so that she shall not rule over her husband, but be subject and obedient to him.

For that reason the wife wears a headdress, that is, the veil on her head, as St. Paul writes in 1. Corinthians in the second chapter, that she is not free but under obedience to her husband.

The wife veils herself with a fine, soft veil, spun and sewn out of pretty, soft flax or linen; and she does not wind a coarse bunch of woven fabric or a dirty cloth around her head or mouth. Why does she do this? So that she speaks fine, lovely, friendly words to her husband and not coarse, filthy, scolding words, as the bad wives do who carry a sword in their mouths and afterward get beaten to the edge of town. Therefore, the wife should have the manner of a grapevine, as it says in the 128th Psalm, for this lets itself be bent and directed with a little band of straw, as the vintner desires. Just so should wives let themselves be guided and taught by their husbands, so that the great and coarse blows and strokes are not used. As pious, obedient wives are accustomed to saying, unbeaten is the best.

That is now part two, what the wife should do in marriage, namely, that she should be subordinate and obedient to her husband and not undertake or do anything without his consent.

13

MATTHIAS GERUNG

Protestant Woodcut

1546

In this woodcut, printed in Germany in 1546, the Protestant artist Matthias Gerung[1] shows Christ at the top deciding who will ascend to heaven and two monstrous demons at the bottom, chained together, dragging people to hell. The demon at the right wears the triple-crowned papal tiara, and the demon at the left the rolled turban worn by the Muslim Ottoman Turks. Both of these were agents of the Antichrist to Protestants. Included in the hell-bound group on the pope's side are men wearing the flat cardinal's hat, the pointed hat of bishops, and the distinctive haircut of monks. Woodcuts such as these adorned inexpensive pamphlets spreading the Protestant message in simple language or were printed (as was this one) as broadsheets, single-sheet posters that were sold alone or in a series. What message about the Catholic clergy and hierarchy does this convey?

[1]mah-TIE-uhs GEH-rung.

Matthias Gerung broadsheet, 1546, from Walter L. Strauss, *The German Single-Leaf Woodcut, 1550–1600* (New York: Abaris Books, 1975), I: 314. Image courtesy of Abaris Books, Norwalk, Conn.

14

IGNATIUS LOYOLA

Spiritual Exercises

1520s

Like Martin Luther, Ignatius Loyola[1] *went through a period of inner turmoil and crisis of conscience but resolved this through a rigorous program of contemplation rather than a new theological approach. At almost exactly the same time that Luther was writing his reformation pamphlets, Loyola was drafting the* Spiritual Exercises, *which set out a training program of structured meditation designed to develop spiritual discipline and allow one to meld one's will with that of God. He wrote them in Spanish; they have since been translated into many different languages and still serve as important tools of spiritual guidance. The* Spiritual Exercises *offered a quick four-week program, under the direction of a spiritual trainer, for those beginning the process of self-discipline. They describe specific exercises and end with a series of rules that assert Catholic doctrine on specific points contested by Protestants. What does the ultimate aim of Loyola's program appear to be? What points of Catholic doctrine does Loyola defend as he sets out expectations for what a believer is supposed to do?*

Introductory Observations

1. By the term "Spiritual Exercises" is meant every method of examination of conscience, of meditation, of contemplation, of vocal and mental prayer, and of other spiritual activities that will be mentioned later. For just as taking a walk, journeying on foot, and running are bodily exercises, so we call Spiritual Exercises every way of preparing and disposing the soul to rid itself of all inordinate attachments, and, after their removal, of seeking and finding the will of God in the disposition of our life for the salvation of our soul. . . .

[1] ig-NEH-shus loy-OH-lah.

Excerpt from *The Spiritual Exercises of St. Ignatius of Loyola*, translated by Louis J. Puhl, S.J. (Chicago: Loyola University, 1951), 1–3, 5, 7, 8–10, 15–17, 43–45, 141, 145–46, 157–58, 160–61. Reprinted with permission of Loyola Press.

4. Four Weeks are assigned to the Exercises given below. This corresponds to the four parts into which they are divided, namely: the first part, which is devoted to the consideration and contemplation of sin; the second part, which is taken up with the life of Christ our Lord up to Palm Sunday inclusive; the third part, which treats of the passion of Christ our Lord; the fourth part, which deals with the Resurrection and Ascension; to this are appended Three Methods of Prayer.

However, it is not meant that each week should necessarily consist of seven or eight days. For it may happen that in the First Week some are slower in attaining what is sought, namely, contrition, sorrow, and tears for sin. Some, too, may be more diligent than others, and some more disturbed and tried by different spirits. It may be necessary, therefore, at times to shorten the Week, and at others to lengthen it. So in our search for the fruit that is proper to the matter assigned, we may have to do the same in all the subsequent Weeks. However, the Exercises should be finished in approximately thirty days.

5. It will be very profitable for the one who is to go through the Exercises to enter upon them with magnanimity and generosity toward his Creator and Lord, and to offer Him his entire will and liberty, that His Divine Majesty may dispose of him and all he possesses according to His most holy will. . . .

18. The Spiritual Exercises must be adapted to the condition of the one who is to engage in them, that is, to his age, education, and talent. Thus exercises that he could not easily bear, or from which he would derive no profit, should not be given to one with little natural ability or of little physical strength. . . .

Similarly, if the one giving the Exercises sees that the exercitant has little aptitude or little physical strength, that he is one from whom little fruit is to be expected, it is more suitable to give him some of the easier exercises as a preparation for confession. . . .

19. One who is educated or talented, but engaged in public affairs or necessary business, should take an hour and a half daily for the Spiritual Exercises. . . .

Ordinarily, the progress made in the Exercises will be greater, the more the exercitant withdraws from all friends and acquaintances, and from all worldly cares. For example, he can leave the house in which he dwelt and choose another house or room in order to live there in as great privacy as possible, so that he will be free to go to Mass and Vespers every day without any fear that his acquaintances will cause any difficulty. . . .

The more the soul is in solitude and seclusion, the more fit it renders itself to approach and be united with its Creator and Lord; and the more closely it is united with Him, the more it disposes itself to receive graces and gifts from the infinite goodness of its God.

24. Daily Particular Examination of Conscience

First, in the morning, immediately on rising, one should resolve to guard carefully against the particular sin or defect with regard to which he seeks to correct or improve himself.

25. Secondly, after dinner, he should ask God our Lord for the grace he desires, that is, to recall how often he has fallen into the particular sin or defect, and to avoid it for the future.

Then follows the first examination. He should demand an account of himself with regard to the particular point which he has resolved to watch in order to correct himself and improve. Let him go over the single hours or periods from the time he arose to the hour and moment of the present examination, and in the first line of the figure given below, make a mark for each time that he has fallen into the particular sin or defect. Then he is to renew his resolution, and strive to amend during the time till the second examination is to be made.

26. Thirdly, after supper, he should make a second examination, going over as before each single hour, commencing with the first examination, and going up to the present one. . . .

[Loyola then provides a chart on which the exercitant can mark the number of times each day he has committed the sin he is trying to avoid.]

65. Fifth Exercise

This is a meditation on hell. . . .

PRAYER.   The preparatory prayer will be as usual.

FIRST PRELUDE.   This is a representation of the place. Here it will be to see in imagination the length, breadth, and depth of hell.

SECOND PRELUDE.   I should ask for what I desire. Here it will be to beg for a deep sense of the pain which the lost suffer, that if because of my faults I forget the love of the eternal Lord, at least the fear of these punishments will keep me from falling into sin.

66. First Point.   This will be to see in imagination the vast fires, and the souls enclosed, as it were, in bodies of fire.

67. Second Point.   To hear the wailing, the howling, cries, and blasphemies against Christ our Lord and against His saints.

68. Third Point.   With the sense of smell to perceive the smoke, the sulphur, the filth, and corruption.

69. Fourth Point.   To taste the bitterness of tears, sadness, and remorse of conscience.

70. Fifth Point.   With the sense of touch to feel the flames which envelop and burn the souls.

71. Colloquy.   Enter into conversation with Christ our Lord. Recall to memory that of those who are in hell, some came there because they did not believe in the coming of Christ; others, though they believed, because they did not keep the Commandments. Divide them all into three classes:

1. Those who were lost before the coming of Christ;
2. Those who were lost during His lifetime;
3. Those who were lost after His life here on earth.

Thereupon, I will give thanks to God our Lord that He has not put an end to my life and permitted me to fall into any of these three classes.
I shall also thank Him for this, that up to this very moment He has shown Himself so loving and merciful to me.
Close with an *Our Father.*

352. Rules for Thinking with the Church

353. 1.   We must put aside all judgment of our own, and keep the mind ever ready and prompt to obey in all things the true Spouse of Christ our Lord, our holy Mother, the hierarchical Church. . . .

356. 4.   We must praise highly religious life, virginity, and continency; and matrimony ought not be praised as much as any of these.

357. 5.   We should praise vows of religion, obedience, poverty, chastity, and vows to perform other works . . . conducive to perfection. . . .

358. 6.   We should show our esteem for the relics of the saints by venerating them and praying to the saints. We should praise visits to

the Station Churches, pilgrimages, indulgences, jubilees, crusade indults, and the lighting of candles in churches.

365. 13.   If we wish to proceed securely in all things, we must hold fast to the following principle: What seems to me white, I will believe black if the hierarchical Church so defines. For I must be convinced that in Christ our Lord, the bridegroom, and in His spouse the Church, only one Spirit holds sway, which governs and rules for the salvation of souls. For it is by the same Spirit and Lord who gave the Ten Commandments that our holy Mother Church is ruled and governed.

366. 14.   Granted that it be very true that no one can be saved without being predestined and without having faith and grace, still we must be very cautious about the way in which we speak of all these things and discuss them with others.

367. 15.   We should not make it a habit of speaking much of predestination. If somehow at times it comes to be spoken of, it must be done in such a way that the people are not led into any error. They are at times misled, so that they say: "Whether I shall be saved or lost, has already been determined, and this cannot be changed whether my actions are good or bad." So they become indolent and neglect the works that are conducive to the salvation and spiritual progress of their souls.

368. 16.   In the same way, much caution is necessary, lest by much talk about faith, and much insistence on it without any distinctions or explanations, occasion be given to the people, whether before or after they have faith informed by charity, to become slothful and lazy in good works.

TERESA OF AVILA

The Way of Perfection

1565

Loyola's Spiritual Exercises *seem to have a male reader in mind, as they assume someone else is cooking the evening dinner while the reader meditates and that only "public affairs or necessary business" might keep a person from having five hours a day to spend on spiritual contemplation. They were clearly read by women, however, some of whom developed their own patterns of devotion. Teresa of Avila[1] had been a contemplative nun and mystic since she was a teenager. When she was in her forties, Teresa felt a call to turn her visions into action, founding a Carmelite convent in her native city in which residents followed strict rules of poverty. Under the direction of her confessor, she wrote her autobiography, describing stages of devotion as the soul ascends toward God. At the same time, she wrote* The Way of Perfection, *explaining why she founded the house and providing guidance for the nuns in their devotional life. Teresa's reforming activities set her in opposition to the city leaders of Avila and many officials in the Spanish church, who thought the life she proposed was too strict for women, particularly those from well-off families. At one point she was even investigated by the Inquisition in an effort to make sure her inspiration came from God and not the devil. Pressure from supporters led the process against her to be dropped, and she spent the last years of her life traveling around Spain, establishing and reforming convents. How does Teresa describe the spread of Protestant ideas? What does she see as the role of cloistered nuns in response to this? She several times describes herself as a "weak" and "wicked" woman. Why do you think she does this? Are there other passages of this text that suggest a different self-evaluation?*

---

[1] AH-vee-luh.

Teresa of Avila, *The Way of Perfection*, edited and translated by E. Allison Peers (New York: Image Books, 1964). Also available online at http://www.ccel.org/ccel/teresa/way/formats/way1.0.pdf (accessed October 1, 2006), 20–22, 25, 27.

Prologue

I know that I am lacking neither in love nor in desire to do all I can to help the souls of my sisters to make great progress in the service of the Lord. It may be that this love, together with my years and the experience which I have of a number of convents, will make me more successful in writing about small matters than learned men can be. For these, being themselves strong and handling other and more important occupations, do not always pay such heed to things which in themselves seem of no importance but which may do great harm to persons as weak as we women are. For the snares laid by the devil for strictly cloistered nuns are numerous and he finds that he needs new weapons if he is to do them harm. I, being a wicked woman, have defended myself but ill, and so I should like my sisters to take warning by me. I shall speak of nothing of which I have no experience, either in my own life or in the observation of others, *or which the Lord has not taught me in prayer. . . .*

Chapter 1

Of the reason which moved me to found this convent in such strict observance.

When this convent was originally founded, for the reasons set down in the book which, as I say, I have already written, and also because of certain wonderful revelations by which the Lord showed me how well He would be served in this house, it was not my intention that there should be so much austerity in external matters, nor that it should have no regular income: on the contrary, I should have liked there to be no possibility of want. I acted, in short, like the weak and wretched woman that I am, although I did so with good intentions and not out of consideration for my own comfort.

At about this time there came to my notice the harm and havoc that were being wrought in France by these Lutherans and the way in which their unhappy sect was increasing. This troubled me very much, and, as though I could do anything, or be of any help in the matter, I wept before the Lord and entreated Him to remedy this great evil. I felt that I would have laid down a thousand lives to save a single one of all the souls that were being lost there. And, seeing that I was a woman, and a sinner, and incapable of doing all I should like in the Lord's service, and as my whole yearning was, and still is, that, as He has so many enemies and so few friends, these last should be trusty ones, I determined to do the little that was in me—namely, to follow the evangelical counsels as perfectly as I could, and to see that these few nuns who are here should do the same, confiding in the great goodness of God, Who never fails to help those who resolve to forsake everything for His sake. As they are all that I have ever painted them as being in my desires, I hoped that their virtues would more than counteract my defects, and I should thus be able to give the Lord some pleasure, and all of us, by busying ourselves in prayer for those who are defenders of the Church, and for the preachers and learned men who defend her, should do everything we could to aid this Lord of mine Who is so much oppressed by those to whom He has shown so much good that it seems as though these traitors would send Him to the Cross again and that He would have nowhere to lay His head. . . .

Oh, my sisters in Christ! Help me to entreat this of the Lord, Who has brought you together here for that very purpose. This is your vocation; this must be your business; these must be your desires; these your tears; these your petitions. Let us not pray for worldly things, my sisters. . . . The world is on fire. Men try to condemn Christ once again, as it were, for they bring a thousand false witnesses against Him. They would raze His Church to the ground—and are we to waste our time upon things which, if God were to grant them, would perhaps bring one soul less to Heaven? No, my sisters, this is no time to treat with God for things of little importance. . . .

Chapter 3

Continues the subject begun in the first chapter and persuades the sisters to busy themselves constantly in beseeching God to help those who work for the Church. Ends with an exclamatory prayer.

Let us now return to the principal reason for which the Lord has brought us together in this house, for which reason I am most desirous that we may be able to please His Majesty. Seeing how great are the evils of the present day and how no human strength will suffice to quench the fire kindled by these heretics (though attempts have been made to organize opposition to them, as though such a great and rapidly spreading evil could be remedied by force of arms), it seems to me that it is like a war in which the enemy has overrun the whole country. . . .

Now why have I said this? So that you may understand, my sisters, that what we have to ask of God is that, in this little castle of ours, inhabited as it is by good Christians, none of us may go over to the enemy. We must ask God, too, to make the captains in this castle or city—that is, the preachers and theologians—highly proficient in the way of the Lord. . . .

It seems over-bold of me to think that I can do anything towards obtaining this. But I have confidence, my Lord, in these servants of Thine who are here, knowing that they neither desire nor strive after anything but to please Thee. For Thy sake they have left the little they possessed, wishing they had more so that they might serve Thee with it. Since Thou, my Creator, art not ungrateful, I do not think Thou wilt fail to do what they beseech of Thee, for when Thou wert in the world, Lord, Thou didst not despise women, but didst always help them and show them great compassion. Thou didst find more faith and no less love in them than in men, and one of them was Thy most sacred Mother, from whose merits we derive merit, and whose habit we wear, though our sins make us unworthy to do so. We can do nothing in public that is of any use to Thee, nor dare we speak of some of the truths over which we weep in secret lest Thou shouldst not hear this our just petition. Yet, Lord I cannot believe this of Thy goodness and righteousness, for Thou art a righteous Judge, not like judges in the world, who, being, after all, men and sons of Adam, refuse to consider any woman's virtue as above suspicion. Yes, my King, but the day will come when all will be known. I am not speaking on my own account, for the whole world is already aware of my wickedness, and I am glad that it should become known; but, when I see what the times are like, I feel it is not right to repel spirits which are virtuous and brave, even though they be the spirits of women.

16

POPE PIUS IV

Injunctum Nobis

1564

Shortly after the final meeting of the Council of Trent, Pope Pius IV issued a profession of faith to be recited publicly by bishops and other clergy. It began with a statement of basic beliefs that all Christians accepted about such things as God's creation of the world and Jesus's life and resurrection. The second part set out specifically Catholic doctrines

Henry Bettenson, ed., *Documents of the Christian Church*, 2nd ed. (London: Oxford University Press, 1963), 267–68.

on every major point of controversy with Protestants, which had recently been affirmed at Trent. This became the standard profession of faith to be recited by converts to Catholicism for centuries. What Catholic doctrines are reasserted here?

I, *N*, with steadfast faith believe and profess each and all the things contained in the Symbol of faith which the holy Roman Church uses, namely . . .

I most firmly acknowledge and embrace the Apostolic and ecclesiastical traditions and other observances and constitutions of the same Church. I acknowledge the sacred Scripture according to that sense which Holy Mother Church has held and holds, to whom it belongs to decide upon the true sense and interpretation of the holy Scriptures, nor will I ever receive and interpret the Scripture except according to the unanimous consent of the Fathers.

I profess also that there are seven sacraments. . . . I embrace and receive each and all of the definitions and declarations of the sacred Council of Trent on Original Sin and Justification.

I profess likewise that true God is offered in the Mass, a proper and propitiatory sacrifice for the living and the dead, and that in the most Holy Eucharist there are truly, really and substantially the body and blood, together with the soul and divinity of Our Lord Jesus Christ, and that a conversion is made of the whole substance of bread into his body and of the whole substance of wine into his blood, which conversion the Catholic Church calls transubstantiation. I also confess that the whole and entire Christ and the true sacrament is taken under the one species alone.

I hold unswervingly that there is a purgatory and that the souls there detained are helped by the intercessions of the faithful; likewise also that the Saints who reign with Christ are to be venerated and invoked; that they offer prayers to God for us and that their relics are to be venerated. I firmly assert that the images of Christ and of the ever-Virgin Mother of God, as also those of other Saints, are to be kept and retained, and that due honour and veneration is to be accorded them; and I affirm that the power of indulgences has been left by Christ in the Church, and that their use is very salutary for Christian people.

I recognize the Holy Catholic and Apostolic Roman Church as the mother and mistress of all churches; and I vow and swear true obedience to the Roman Pontiff, the successor of blessed Peter, the chief of the Apostles and the representative of Jesus Christ.

I accept and profess, without doubting, the traditions, definitions and declarations of the sacred Canons and Ecumenical Councils and especially those of the holy Council of Trent; and at the same time I condemn, reject and anathematize all things contrary thereto, and all heresies condemned, rejected and anathematized by the Church. This true Catholic Faith (without which no one can be in a state of salvation), which at this time I of my own will profess and truly hold, I, *N*, vow and swear, God helping me, most constantly to keep and confess entire and undefiled to my life's last breath, and that I will endeavour, as far as in me shall lie, that it be held, taught and preached by my subordinates or by those who shall be placed under my care: so help me God and these Holy Gospels of God.

17

JOHN CALVIN

Institutes of the Christian Religion
1536

In the later sixteenth century the most influential form of Protestantism was that inspired by John Calvin. Calvin's Institutes of the Christian Religion, *which he revised and expanded many times, brings together Protestant doctrine and thought in a systematic way. In the* Institutes, *Calvin stressed human sinfulness and redemptive grace through Jesus Christ. In this section, how does Calvin view God's power in determining who will achieve eternal salvation?*

The covenant of life is not preached equally to all, and among those to whom it is preached, does not always meet with the same reception. This diversity displays the unsearchable depth of the divine judgment, and is without doubt subordinate to God's purpose of eternal election. But it is plainly owing to the mere pleasure of God that salvation is spontaneously offered to some, while others have no access to it,

John Calvin, *Institutes of the Christian Religion*, translated by Henry Beveridge (Edinburgh: Calvin Translation Society, 1845), 2:529, 534, 540.

great and difficult questions immediately arise, questions which are inexplicable, when just views are not entertained concerning election and predestination. . . .

By predestination we mean the eternal decree of God, by which he determined with himself whatever he wished to happen with regard to every man. All are not created on equal terms, but some are preordained to eternal life, others to eternal damnation; and, accordingly, as each has been created for one or other of these ends, we say that he has been predestined to life or to death. . . .

We say, then, that Scripture clearly proves this much, that God by his eternal and immutable counsel determined once for all those whom it was his pleasure one day to admit to salvation, and those whom, on the other hand, it was his pleasure to doom to destruction. We maintain that this counsel, as regards the elect, is founded on his free mercy, without any respect to human worth, while those whom he dooms to destruction are excluded from access to life by a just and blameless, but at the same time incomprehensible judgment. In regard to the elect, we regard calling as the evidence of election, and justification as another symbol of its manifestation, until it is fully accomplished by the attainment of glory. But as the Lord seals his elect by calling and justification, so by excluding the reprobate either from the knowledge of his name or the sanctification of his Spirit, he by these marks in a manner discloses the judgment which awaits them.

18

JOHN CALVIN

Ordinances for the Regulation of Churches

1547

Though nothing could change the "terrible decree"—Calvin's own words—of predestination, many people were attracted to Calvin's notion that proper moral conduct could fulfill God's will in the world. Calvin's

James H. Robinson, ed., *Translations and Reprints from the Original Sources of European History* (Philadelphia: University of Pennsylvania, 1902), 3:10–11.

writings attracted the attention of city leaders in Geneva, who had just thrown out their bishop and were setting up new city and church governance structures. They asked for Calvin's assistance in this, and he spent the rest of his life—with one short break—in Geneva transforming the city into a community based on his religious principles. A well-disciplined city, like a well-disciplined individual, might be seen as evidence of God's decision. A number of ordinances regulated public and family life, and various institutions enforced these laws, of which the most powerful was the Consistory, a group of pastors and laymen charged with investigating and disciplining deviations from proper doctrine and conduct. Given the actions prohibited in these ordinances, how would you describe ideal Christian behavior, in Calvin's eyes?

Blasphemy

Whoever shall have blasphemed, swearing by the body or by the blood of our Lord, or in similar manner, he shall be made to kiss the earth for the first offence; for the second to pay 5 sous,[1] and for the third 6 sous, and for the last offence be put in the pillory for one hour.

Drunkenness

1. That no one shall invite another to drink under penalty of 3 sous.
2. That taverns shall be closed during the sermon, under penalty that the tavern-keeper shall pay 3 sous, and whoever may be found therein shall pay the same amount.
3. If any one be found intoxicated he shall pay for the first offence 3 sous and shall be remanded to the consistory; for the second offence he shall be held to pay the same sum of 6 sous, and for the third 10 sous and be put in prison.

Songs and Dances

If any one sing immoral, dissolute or outrageous songs, or dance the *virollet* or other dance, he shall be put in prison for three days and then sent to the consistory.

---

[1] *sou*: A small coin.

Usury

That no one shall take upon interest or profit more than five percent, upon penalty of confiscation of the principal and of being condemned to make restitution as the case may demand.

Games

That no one shall play at any dissolute game or at any game whatsoever it may be, neither for gold nor silver nor for any excessive stake, upon penalty of 5 sous and forfeiture of stake played for. . . .

Concerning the Celebration of the Marriage

That the parties at the time when they are to be married shall go modestly to the church, without drummers and minstrels, preserving an order and gravity becoming to Christians; and this before the last stroke of the bell, in order that the marriage blessing may be given before the sermon. If they are negligent and come too late they shall be sent away.

3

Africa and Southwest Asia: Politics and Mysticism in Islam and Judaism

BACKGROUND

In the seventh and eighth centuries, Arab followers of the Prophet Muhammad conquered much of southwest Asia, North Africa, and the Iberian peninsula of Europe. These areas slowly converted to Islam. In subsequent centuries Islam spread further: into East and West Africa, South and Central Asia, and mainland and island Southeast Asia. By 1500 the Islamic world stretched from the Atlantic Ocean to the South China Sea, and various rulers used Islam as a means of strengthening their power. Islam could divide as well as unify, however, and the early modern period saw major struggles between Islamic empires that were political and religious enemies. Religious developments in the Islamic world were not simply a matter of power politics, however. The mystical movement known as Sufism offered Muslim believers guidance in coming nearer to God and in pious daily living. Judaism, whose adherents often found refuge from Christian persecution in Muslim territories, also harbored a tradition of mysticism known as the Kabbalah[1] that offered a distinct path to religious understanding.

Traders brought Islam across the Sahara into West Africa, where merchants and rulers found its teachings attractive and aspects of Islamic administrative, economic, and legal traditions useful. In the fourteenth century, the ruler of the Mali Empire, Mansa Musa, made the pilgrimage to Mecca expected of pious Muslims, and returned eager to promote Islam. He ordered the construction of larger and more impressive mosques, and brought scholars from Cairo and Baghdad, the oldest centers of Islamic learning, to Timbuktu, his capital. Timbuktu became an important center of Islamic scholarship and book production; manuscript books joined salt and gold as the city's most important commodities.

[1] kah-BAH-lah.

The fortunes of Islam waxed and waned in early modern Timbuktu. In 1468, the city was conquered by Sunni Ali Ber (ruled 1464–1492), the founder of the Songhay Empire, which succeeded the Mali Empire as the largest in West Africa. Though Sunni Ali Ber was officially a Muslim, he thought that the scholars of Timbuktu, many of whom were Arabs from North Africa and southwest Asia, did not pay enough respect to the African religions that predated Islam in West Africa and which many of his own people still followed. Sunni Ali threatened to arrest the Timbuktu scholars, and many of them fled the city, taking their manuscripts with them. But the scholars returned when one of Sunni Ali's generals, Askia the Great, took over the throne in 1493. Askia returned to the strong support for Islam that earlier rulers had shown. He promoted the building of mosques and schools and the writing of books on Muslim history and law, consulted Islamic scholars on legal and political matters, and made the pilgrimage to Mecca.

One of the scholars Askia consulted was the celebrated North African reformer Muhammad al-Maghili (d. 1503), who was born in the thriving commercial city of Tlemcen in what is now Algeria. Al-Maghili studied Islamic texts and law with a series of notable scholars and became particularly concerned with the status of non-Muslims living in Muslim states. Muslim law prescribed the proper treatment of Jews and Christians—fellow "Peoples of the Book" who also worshipped one God and acknowledged many of the same prophets. They could not bear arms and were expected to pay special taxes but were not required to convert, and in most parts of the Muslim world they lived peacefully. Al-Maghili developed very different ideas. He thought that Jews living in North Africa did not show the proper respect owed Muslim authorities, and he preached and wrote vicious works against them, calling for the destruction of their synagogues and expulsion. Some Jews had become prosperous through the trans-Saharan trade, sparking economic resentment much like that in Christian Europe at the same time, and al-Maghili's preaching found an audience. His actions led to riots and massacres of Jews in several North African cities in the early 1490s. In the later 1490s al-Maghili traveled south to the states of western Africa, where he provided advice to rulers, including Askia the Great, on matters of Islamic law and tradition. He apparently succeeded in having Jews prohibited from entering the Songhay Empire and then turned his attention to how followers of traditional African religions were to be handled. On this as well, he advocated a strict interpretation of Islamic law, recommending death or slavery, particularly for those who claimed to be Muslim but still followed traditional practices. (See Document 19.)

Elsewhere in the Islamic world rulers' measures against those with different religious practices and beliefs were directed more at fellow Muslims than at Jews or the followers of traditional religions. In southwest Asia, the Ottoman and Safavid Empires became bitter political and religious opponents. Their religious division originated in the years immediately following the death of the Prophet Muhammad in 632. Neither Muhammad himself nor his revelations as written in the Qur'an gave clear guidance about how his successors were to be chosen. In 632, a group of Muhammad's closest followers elected Abu Bakr as *caliph*,[2] a word meaning successor. Abu Bakr was a close friend of the Prophet's and a member of a small tribe affiliated with the Prophet's tribe. This election set a precedent for the ratification of the subsequent caliphs.

The fourth caliph, Ali, claimed the caliphate because of his blood ties with Muhammad—he was his cousin and son-in-law—and because the Prophet had designated him as *imam* or leader. Ali was assassinated in 661 shortly after becoming caliph, and his supporters began to assert that he should rightly have been the first caliph and that all other caliphs were usurpers. These supporters of Ali—termed *Shi'ites* or *Shi'a* from Arabic terms meaning supporters or partisans of Ali—saw him and subsequent imams as the divinely inspired leaders of the community. Shi'ites thus often had messianic hopes for the future and were devoted to particular imams believed to have special religious powers. One group of Shi'ites, known as Twelvers, held that the twelfth imam after Ali had gone into hiding to escape persecution but would one day return and take over proper religious authority. The larger body of Muslims—termed *Sunnis*, a word derived from *Sunna*, the traditional beliefs and practices of the community—accepted the first elections and relied more on the advice of the group of scholars and jurists who studied sacred texts (a group known as the *ulama*) than on charismatic imams for spiritual guidance.

The Ottoman Turks accepted Sunni Islam. The name *Ottoman* was taken from Osman Bey, the capable leader of a group of Turks who began to expand their territory in Asia Minor in the thirteenth century. Ottoman forces entered Europe in 1345, and took Constantinople in 1453, which they renamed Istanbul and made the capital of the Ottoman Empire. In 1517, Sultan Selim I "the Grim" (ruled 1512–1520) invaded the Mamluk Sultanate, which ruled Syria and much of

[2]KAY-lif.

North Africa, and within a few months had taken the entire eastern Mediterranean, Egypt, North Africa, and the Arabian peninsula. These conquered territories included all the holy places in Islam. To reinforce his authority Selim began to refer to himself using the traditional title of "caliph," which implied a measure of both political and spiritual authority over Sunni Muslims everywhere. Over the next century the Ottomans advanced further, and by 1600 they were rulers of about a third of Europe, half the shores of the Mediterranean, and most of southwest Asia.

Selim's expansion put the Ottomans into direct conflict with another Muslim Empire, that of the Safavids, centered in Persia, or present-day Iran. The Safavids took their name from Safi al-Din (1252–1334), the leader of a Muslim religious brotherhood (*tariqa*), one of many groups vying for control in southwest Asia after the disintegration of the Mongol Empire. In 1499, Ismail (?–1524), a teenager who was the hereditary leader of this brotherhood, began assembling an army and asserting power. Several years later he proclaimed himself ruler, or shah, of Iran. He declared that his subjects would from that point on all accept Twelver Shi'ism. Many of his followers, which included large numbers of nomadic Turks, viewed him as the hidden imam, and some even saw him as god incarnate, so they fiercely supported his decisions. Many people in Iran at this point were Sunni, however, and some fled to neighboring Sunni lands for asylum.

One of those lands was the Ottoman Empire, where the rulers watched the rise of the Safavids with apprehension, worried about their growing military power and support for the spread of Shi'ite teachings among people within the Ottoman Empire. Each side declared that the other perverted the true teachings of the Prophet. (See Document 20.) Ottoman forces attacked the Safavid Empire, and fighting continued off and on for centuries, with each side viewing adherents of the other branch of Islam within its own borders as political opponents as well as heretics. In the Safavid Empire, Ismail and his successors enforced Shi'ite beliefs through force and through learning; they persecuted Sunnis but also brought in Shi'ite scholars from elsewhere in the Muslim world to establish schools. In the Ottoman Empire, officials arrested and charged people with being Safavid sympathizers, testing their loyalty by demanding they say Sunni prayers and affirm the early caliphs as the true successors to Muhammad. In 1537, Süleyman I ordered that mosques should be built in every village and that all men should be expected to attend Sunni prayer services regularly. His immediate successors created a more centralized system of government-run schools, courts, and mosques, granting the chief legal official in the empire a new title as *Sheyhulislam*[3] or Sheikh of Islam. The Sheyhulislam became the head of the religious-legal establishment, with the power to standardize interpretation of doctrine and the implementation of Islamic law across the entire Ottoman Empire, a transformation that was truly unprecedented.

The strength of the Safavid Empire lay not simply in its armies and scholars, but also in its connections with the mystical movement in Islam known as *Sufism*.[4] Beginning in the eighth century, some Muslim thinkers increasingly emphasized seeking the truth and gaining awareness of God through contemplation, meditation, prayer, and other spiritual practices. Through these personal devotional activities, Sufi adherents sought to deepen their love of God, free themselves from concern with worldly affairs, and progress along a path of increasing spiritual awareness; their goal was to lose themselves in God or become one with God, a process that could involve sudden flashes of insight and intuition as well as regular devotional practice. The thirteenth-century Sufi poet and scholar Rumi, for example, focused intensely on the unity of God (a central concept for all Muslims), purity of the heart, and the progress of the soul through life and death. He thought that music, dancing, and poetry could help people achieve greater spiritual awareness and bring them closer to God. (See Document 21.) Sufism could have developed into a separate branch of Islam, but most Sufis taught that those who gained knowledge of God through direct experience or mystical insights still had to obey Muslim law (the *shari'a*), and Sufism became part of orthodox Islam. Sufi teachings were accepted and spread by individuals who were both Sunnis and Shi'as.

Early Sufi masters, called sheikhs,[5] were often wandering visionaries, venerated for their wisdom, ecstatic statements, and austere lifestyle. Non-Muslims occasionally attended the mystical sessions of Sufi masters and are reported to have been converted to Islam through their teachings. Some Sufi masters came to be viewed as saints, holy persons who were particularly close to God. The Sufi historian Abdulwahhab b. Ahmad al-Sharani wrote biographies of many of the saints in the 1550s, recording their words and deeds. (See Document 22.) Sufi saints were the focus of individualized popular devotion; as in Christianity, people read or heard stories about their lives and miracles, prayed to them for assistance, and made pilgrimages to their shrines. Some Sufi shrines had, in fact, been Christian shrines earlier, and a few

---

[3] shay-kuhl-iz-LAHM.
[4] SOO-fizm.
[5] SHAYKS.

places were sacred to both Christianity and Islam. Criticism of Sufism also had parallels with Christianity. As did Christian humanists and Protestant reformers in Europe, learned Muslim leaders sometimes objected to the emotional rituals and pilgrimages favored by Sufis and their adherents, arguing that they led people away from the essentials of Islam. (See Document 23.)

Opposition to Sufi teachings rarely had much effect, however. Not only were exuberant Sufi ceremonies generally more popular than the more formal and reserved services in mosques, but beginning in the twelfth century some Sufi masters organized religious brotherhoods that promoted pious living but without the extreme asceticism of the original saints. These Sufi brotherhoods became not only devotional groups, but important social, political, and economic institutions; the brotherhood of the Safavids, as we have seen, became the rulers of an empire. (Though, ironicially, once they came to power the Safavids persecuted many Sufi brotherhoods.) The Ottoman Turks also originated in a Sufi brotherhood, the Mevlevis, founded by the followers of Rumi. By the early modern period most Muslim men, especially those who lived in cities, belonged to a brotherhood, each with its own rituals and ceremonies, just as many Christian men in Catholic Europe and Mexico belonged to a confraternity. (The word *confraternity*, is, in fact, a Latinized version of *brotherhood*.) Some Sufi brotherhoods included women, providing a religious community and role not available elsewhere in Islam, but the majority of members were men, and Sufi literature largely reflects the male experience.

More individualized and mystical forms of piety were not limited to Muslims in the Islamic world, but could also be found among Jews who lived in Muslim-held territories. (There was no Jewish empire or state in the early modern world, and nowhere did Jews have political authority over non-Jews, so there are no sources from Jewish authorities that parallel Documents 19 and 20.) Jewish mysticism centers on the Kabbalah, texts that originated in the thirteenth century but looked back to much older traditions. The Kabbalah offers mystical understandings of the nature of God, the origins of evil, the meaning of religious texts and ceremonies, the various aspects of the human soul, and a range of other topics. Kabbalah centers especially on ten qualities of the Divine known as the *sefirot*, including wisdom, compassion, sincerity, and mercy, which humans are able to experience through prayer, study, rituals, and contemplation.

Kabbalah originated in Spain and southern France, but in the early modern period Kabbalistic writings and practices spread throughout the Mediterranean, largely as the result of Christian persecution of Jews. In 1492, King Ferdinand of Aragon and Queen Isabella of Castile conquered Granada, the last remaining Muslim state in the Iberian peninsula. Continuing their drive for religious uniformity in their realm, they ordered all Jews in Spain to convert to Christianity or leave, and perhaps as many as 200,000 left. Some went to the Low Countries or Italy, but many went to Muslim lands. As noted earlier, some of the cities in North and West Africa had also expelled Jews, but the rulers of the Ottoman Empire remained tolerant. As their empire expanded, the Ottomans required conquered peoples to pay taxes but allowed them to keep their own laws and traditions, including religion. Religious communities paid taxes, but they could practice their religion openly, retain their own systems of religious law, and teach their children.

With the diaspora of Spanish Jews after the expulsion of 1492, many Kabbalists settled in the village of Safed in Palestine (present-day Israel) in the Ottoman Empire. In the 1530s Safed became a center of study and intense religious practice under the leadership of rabbis such as Moses Cordovero and Isaac Luria. Here they developed new systems of spiritual practices, mystical ceremonies, and guides to behavior based on the Kabbalah. (See Documents 24 and 25.) Groups studying and practicing Lurianic Kabbalah were organized in many Jewish communities in the Ottoman Empire and in Europe, devoted to intense prayer, moral behavior, interior individual piety, and the study of sacred texts. (See Document 26.) They remained a minority within Judaism and did not become a broad sociocultural development the way Sufi brotherhoods did in Islam, but in many of their activities as well as their mystical approach to God, Kabbalistic groups paralleled Sufi brotherhoods.

DOCUMENTS

Developments in early modern Islam and Judaism generated many different types of sources. Conflicts involving different interpretations of Muslim tradition are discussed in official government documents, formal legal treatises, and other works by the trained legal scholars of the *ulama*. In West Africa, the scholars and students of Timbuktu produced and bought huge numbers of manuscripts, of which about 700,000 survive in and around Timbuktu today. In his multivolume *Description of Africa*, first published in 1550, Leo Africanus, a Spanish Muslim later baptized as a Christian and employed by the pope, wrote of Timbuktu: "Here are great stores of doctors, judges, priests, and other learned men, that are bountifully maintained at the king's cost and charges. Hither are brought diverse manuscripts or written books, which are sold for more money than any other merchandise."[6]

Sufi mystical teachings were spread orally among adherents, but also through written works of various types, which were frequently translated, copied, and incorporated in the works of later writers. Some Sufi devotional works contained illustrations. Muslim authorities in many areas regarded representation of the human form as unacceptable, so illustrations were limited to natural designs, geometric forms, and elaborate calligraphy. This ban was not enforced in the Safavid Empire, however, and Shah Ismail and his successors patronized artists and supported the production of exquisitely illustrated books that portray Iranian history and religious practices.

Within Judaism, the most influential center of study and practice of the mysticism of the Kabbalah in the early modern period was Safed. Writings from Safed were published on what were the earliest printing presses in the Middle East.

The four main themes outlined in the Introduction emerge in the documents in this chapter. The role of political elites in religion is discussed in several documents. How would you compare the attitude of al-Maghili (Document 19) toward those in Songhay who practiced traditional religions with that of Sultan Selim I (Document 20) toward Shah Ismail's Shi'a Islam? How might their attitudes have been shaped by the political contexts surrounding these interactions? Sufism and Kaballah were both mystical movements in which believers sought unity with God. How do the Sufi defenders of sacred whirling (Documents 21 and 23) and Moses Cordovero (Document 24) describe this process of becoming one with God? What parallels do you see in the language, practices, and understandings of the divine in Sufism (Documents 21–23) and Kaballah (Documents 24–26)? In the practices expected in a believer? What role do religious authorities appear to play in these movements? (For questions that relate these sources to those in other chapters in the book, see p. 163.)

(For questions that relate these sources to those in other chapters in the book, see p. 163.)

---

[6]Leo Africanus, *The History and Description of Africa*, translated by John Pory, Hakluyt Society, vol. 94 (New York: Burt Franklin, 1896), 3:825. Since 2000 the Timbuktu Educational Foundation has been working to restore and preserve these manuscripts, and to publish and translate the most significant of them. See the organization's Web site: http://www.timbuktufoundation.org.

19

The Replies of Muhammad al-Maghili to the Questions of Askia al-Hajj Muhammad

1498

In many of his writings, the prominent legal scholar Muhammad al-Maghili[1] was concerned with the status of non-Muslims living in Muslim states. In the 1490s he traveled to the states of western Africa, where he provided advice to rulers on matters of Islamic law and tradition. He wrote a treatise of advice for Muhammad Rumfa (ruled 1463–1499), the ruler of the Hausa city-state of Kano, and shortly afterwards another for Askia al-Hajj[2] Muhammad, the ruler of the Songhay Empire. This was couched in the form of questions posed by Askia Muhammad with replies by al-Maghili, but there is no way of knowing if these were an actual conversation or if al-Maghili simply wrote them this way after his discussions with Askia Muhammad. In this section of the dialogue, al-Maghili discusses those who claim to be Muslim but also follow traditional African religions. How does he advise Askia to handle them? What does al-Maghili view as the proper role of political authorities in handling religion?

Your statement: I entered these lands after Sunni 'Alī, who had amassed wealth and slaves from diverse sources, and I took possession of all of that. Then I released everyone who claimed that he was a free Muslim and a large number of them went off. Then after that I asked about the circumstances of some of them and about their country and behold they pronounced the shahāda:[3] "There is no god save God; Muhammad is the Messenger of God." But in spite of that they believe that there are beings who can bring them benefit or do them harm other than God, Mighty and Exalted is He. They have idols and

[1] ahl MAH-geh-lee.
[2] AHS-kee-yah al-HAHDGE.
[3] shahāda: The Muslim statement of faith.

they say: "The fox has said so and so and thus it will be," and "If the thing is thus then it will be so and so." They venerate certain trees and make sacrifices to them. They have their shrines . . . and they do not appoint a ruler or undertake any matter either great or small except at the command of the custodians of their shrines.

So I admonished them to give up all that and they refused to do so without the use of force. Does this render them unbelievers and make it lawful for them to be put to death and their property to be seized if they persist in this—although they say with their tongues: "There is no god save God; Muḥammad is the Messenger of God"? And Sunni 'Alī never demanded profession of Islam from them nor anything else; he merely treated them as he treated the Muslims. I have now made clear to them that they should abandon what they are doing. So if they do not abandon it, what should I do to them?

The reply—and God it is who directs to the right way—is that dominion belongs to God entirely and judgement belongs to God both in the beginning and at the last, so give thanks for God's bounty to you and fear Him concerning those matters over which He has given you power and with which He has charged you.

Know, then, that Sunni 'Alī bore his burden on his [own] neck and earned his just deserts [from God] in so doing until his allotted life span expired. Then that burden was cast down before you and it was you who took it up. Therefore, in bearing it, acquire for yourself that from which blessing may be hoped and whose result will be to your praise in this world and the next. Say not, then, of an evil to which you could put an end today: "This does not concern me since I did not commit it; it was the work of another." For every course of action taken by another which subsequently comes under your control, if it is good then uphold it and if it is evil then put an end to it, even though it has persisted for a long time. For dominion belongs to God and it is incumbent upon you to set aright all that is passed on to you.

In the light of this, your action in setting free all those who claimed to be free Muslims was correct. . . .

As for the people whose conduct you described, they are polytheists without doubt, for in accordance with the literal interpretation of the ruling, one may be adjudged an unbeliever for less than that, as we explained in the preceding Question. There is no doubt that *jihād*[4] against them is more fitting and worthy than *jihād* against [born] unbelievers who do not say: "There is no god save God; Muḥammad

---

[4]*jihād*: Struggle.

is the Messenger of God," since those whom you describe have confounded the truth with falsehood in such a way as to mislead many of the ignorant Muslims so that they become unbelievers without realizing it. They are more worthy [to be made the object] of a *jihād* than the [outright] unbelievers whom no Muslim would imitate.

So make *jihād* against them, killing their men and enslaving their women and children and seizing their property in accordance with what we put forward in the Reply to the previous Question. If they persist in their polytheism, burn the custodians of their shrines and their gods. . . . Every one of them whom you release because he claims to be a free Muslim, then it becomes plain to you that he is an unbeliever, reduce him to slavery again and seize his property, unless he repents and becomes a good Muslim, in which case leave him alone as you did at first. "Whoever leaves aside something for the sake of God, God will compensate with something better than it. To God belong the coffers of the Heavens and the earth, though the hypocrites comprehend not."[5]

[5] Qur'an 63:7.

20

SULTAN SELIM I AND SHAH ISMAIL

Letters

1514

In 1499, Ismail,[1] the leader of the Safavid Sufi brotherhood in Persia, proclaimed himself ruler and declared that all his subjects would from that point on accept the Shi'ite interpretation of Islam. Many Sunni Muslims fled to neighboring countries, including the Ottoman Empire, where Sultan Selim[2] I opposed the Safavids' growing military power and their interpretation of Muslim tradition. Both rulers had expansionary

[1] ihs-MAH-eel.
[2] seh-LEEM.

"Letters from Selim and Ismail," translated by John E. Woods in *The Islamic World*, ed. William H. McNeill and Marilyn Robinson Waldman (New York: Oxford University Press, 1973), 338–44.

aims and attacked various other Muslim states on their borders. By 1514, they confronted one another directly and prepared for war. Shortly before fighting began, Sultan Selim sent Shah Ismail several letters, to which Ismail responded. What does their correspondence indicate about each ruler's attitudes toward the other's understanding of Islam? As rulers, what role do they see themselves having in enforcing religious law?

I. Selîm to Ismâ'îl (undated, ca. 1514)

"It is from Solomon and it is: 'In the Name of God, the Merciful, the Compassionate. Rise not up against me, but come to me in surrender.'"
[Qur'ân XXVII:30–31]

God's blessings upon the best of his creatures, Muhammad, his family, and his companions all.

"This is a Scripture We have sent down, blessed; so follow it, and be godfearing; haply so you will find mercy." [Qur'ân VI:156]

This missive which is stamped with the seal of victory and which is, like inspiration descending from the heavens, witness to the verse "We never chastise until We send forth a Messenger" [Qur'ân XVII: 15] has been graciously issued by our most glorious majesty—we who are the Caliph of God Most High in this world, far and wide; the proof of the verse "And what profits men abides in the earth" [Qur'ân XIII:17] the Solomon of Splendor, the Alexander of eminence; haloed in victory, Farîdûn triumphant; slayer of the wicked and the infidel, guardian of the noble and the pious; the warrior in the Path, the defender of the Faith; the champion, the conqueror; the lion, son and grandson of the lion; standard-bearer of justice and righteousness, Sultân Selîm Shâh, son of Sultân Bayezîd, son of Sultân Muhammad Khân—and is addressed to the ruler of the kingdom of the Persians, the possessor of the land of tyranny and perversion, the captain of the vicious, the chief of the malicious, the usurping Darius[3] of the time, the malevolent Zahhâk[4] of the age, the peer of Cain, Prince Ismâ'îl.

It has been heard repeatedly that you have subjected the upright community of Muhammad (Prayers and salutations upon its founder!) to your devious will, that you have undermined the firm foundation of

---

[3] *Darius*: An ancient Persian king who took over the throne by violence.
[4] *Zahhâk*: A mythological evil king.

the Faith, that you have unfurled the banner of oppression in the cause of aggression, that you no longer uphold the commandments and prohibitions of the Divine Law, that you have incited your abominable Shî'î faction to unsanctified sexual union and to the shedding of innocent blood, that like they "Who listen to falsehood and consume the unlawful" [Qur'ân V:42] you have given ear to idle deceitful words and have eaten that which is forbidden:

> He has laid waste to mosques, as it is said,
> Constructing idol temples in their stead,

that you have rent the noble stuff of Islâm with the hand of tyranny, and that you have called the Glorious Qur'ân the myths of the Ancients. The rumor of these abominations has caused your name to become like that of Hârith deceived by Satan.

Indeed, as both the *fatwas*[5] of distinguished *'ulamâ'*[6] who base their opinion on reason and tradition alike and the consensus of the Sunnî community agree that the ancient obligation of extirpation, extermination, and expulsion of evil innovation must be the aim of our exalted aspiration, for "Religious zeal is a victory for the Faith of God the Beneficent"; then, in accordance with the words of the Prophet (Peace upon him!) "Whosoever introduces evil innovation into our order must be expelled" and "Whosoever does aught against our order must be expelled," action has become necessary and exigent. Thus, when the Divine Decree of Eternal Destiny commended the eradication of the infamously wicked infidels into our capable hands, we set out for their lands like ineluctable fate itself to enforce the order "Leave not upon the earth of the Unbelievers even one." [Qur'ân LXXI:26] If God almighty wills, the lightning of our conquering sword shall uproot the untamed bramble grown to great heights in the path of the refulgent Divine Law and shall cast them down upon the dust of abjectness to be trampled under the hooves of our legions, for "They make the mightiest of its inhabitants abased. Even so they too will do" [Qur'ân XXVII:34]; the thunder of our avenging mace shall dash out the muddled brains of the enemies of the Faith as rations for the lion-hearted *ghâzîs*.[7] "And those who do wrong shall surely know by what overthrowing they will be overthrown." [Qur'ân XXVI:227]. . . .

---

[5]*fatwa*: Religious opinion on Islamic law.
[6]*ulamâ/ulema*: Group of Islamic legal scholars.
[7]*ghâzî*: Islamic warrior.

But "Religion is Counsel," and should you turn the countenance of submission to the *qibla*[8] of bliss and the Ka'ba[9] of hope—our angelic threshhold, the refuge of the noble—moreover, should you lift up the hand of oppression from the heads of your subjects ruined by tyranny and sedition, should you take up a course of repentance, become like one blameless and return to the sublime straight path of the Sunna of Muhammad (Prayers and salutations upon him and God's satisfaction upon his immaculate family and his rightly-guided companions all!). For "My companions are like the stars: whomever you choose to follow, you will be guided aright." And finally should you consider your lands and their people part of the well-protected Ottoman state, then shall you be granted our royal favor and our imperial patronage.

He whose face touches the dust of my threshold in submission
Will be enveloped in the shadow of my favor and my justice.

How great the happiness of him who complies with this!

On the other hand, if your evil, seditious habits have become a part of your nature, that which has become essential can never again be accidental.

What avail sermons to the black-hearted?

Then, with the support and assistance of God, I will crown the head of every gallows tree with the head of a crown-wearing Sûfî and clear that faction from the face of the earth. . . .

II. Ismâ'îl to Selîm (undated, ca. 1514)

May his godly majesty, the refuge of Islâm, the might of the kingdom, he upon whom God looks with favor, the champion of the sultanate and of the state, the hero of the faith and of the earth, Sultân Selîm Shâh (God grant him immortal state and eternal happiness!) accept this affectionate greeting and this friendly letter, considering it a token of our good will.

Now to begin: Your honored letters have arrived one after another, for "No sooner has a thing doubled than it has tripled." Their contents,

---

[8] *qibla*: Direction one faces when praying, for Muslims.
[9] *Ka'ba*: Holiest building in Islam, in Mecca.

although indicative of hostility, are stated with boldness and vigor. The latter gives us much enjoyment and pleasure, but we are ignorant of the reason for the former. In the time of your late blessed father (May God enlighten his proof!) when our royal troops passed through the lands of Rûm to chastise the impudence of 'Alâ' al-Dawla Dhû'l-Qadr, complete concord and friendship was shown on both sides. Moreover, when your majesty was governor at Trebizond [i.e., before his accession] there existed perfect mutual understanding. Thus, now, the cause of your resentment and displeasure yet remains unknown. If political necessity has compelled you on this course, then may your problems soon be solved.

> Dispute may fire words to such a heat
> That ancient houses be consumed in flames.

The intention of our inaction in this regard is twofold:

(1) Most of the inhabitants of the land of Rûm are followers of our forefathers (May God the All-Forgiving King have mercy upon them!).

(2) We have always loved the *ghâzî*-titled Ottoman house and we do not wish the outbreak of sedition and turmoil once again as in the time of Tîmûr.

Why should we then take umbrage at these provocations? We shall not.

> The mutual hostility of kings is verily an ancient rite.

> Should one hold the bride of worldly rule too close,
> His lips those of the radiant sword will kiss.

Nevertheless, there is no cause for improper words: indeed, those vain, heretical imputations are the mere fabrications of the opium-clouded minds of certain secretaries and scribes. We therefore think that our delayed reply was not completely without cause for we have now dispatched our honored personal companion and servant Shâh Qulî Âghâ (May he be sustained!) with a golden casket stamped with the royal seal and filled with a special preparation for their use should they deem it necessary. May he soon arrive so that with assistance from above the mysteries concealed behind the veil of fate might be disclosed. But one should always exercise free judgment not bound solely by the words of others and always keep in view that in the end regrets avail him naught.

At this writing we were engaged upon the hunt near Isfahân; we now prepare provisions and our troops for the coming campaign. In all friendship we say do what you will.

> Bitter experience has taught that in this world of trial
> He who falls upon the house of 'Alî always falls.

Kindly give our ambassador leave to travel unmolested. "No soul laden bears the load of another." [Qur'ân VI:164; LIII:38]

When war becomes inevitable, hesitation and delay must be set aside, and one must think on that which is to come. Farewell.

21

Mystical Dance of a Sufi Brotherhood

1500s

This illustration from a manuscript made in the Safavid Empire shows members of a Sufi[1] brotherhood in a devotional dance. Some Sufi brotherhoods, particularly those of the Mevlevi brotherhood, focused on spinning until one was "a drop of wine in the ocean of God's love." Mevlevi sacred texts were generally written in Persian, a language that originated in Iran, but later spread to the Ottoman Empire as well. Many of the most important poets and composers in the Ottoman Empire were Mevlevis, and even Sultan Selim I composed poetry in Persian. Meanwhile his bitter enemy Shah Ismail (see Document 20) wrote poetry in Turkish, and many of his most devoted followers spoke Turkish. Religious differences were thus more important than language in separating Safavids and Ottomans. Given Sufi aims of a mystical union with God, why might spinning have been a devotional activity? Western Europeans referred to Sufi dancers as "whirling dervishes," from the Persian word darvish, *meaning an ascetic. What cultural judgments are suggested by this phrase?*

[1]SOO-fee.

22

ABDULWAHHAB B. AHMAD AL-SHARANI

Qualities of a Sufi Saint

ca. 1560

Abdulwahhab[1] b. Ahmad al-Sharani[2] (1491–1565) was a Sufi historian and scholar living in Egypt during the time that the Ottomans conquered the area. He was himself a mystic and wrote extensive biographies of Sufi leaders, which remain popular reading among Sufis in Egypt today. His writings include long passages from the works of important earlier Sufi sheikhs, many of which are known only through al-Sharani's books. Here he quotes from the thirteenth-century mystical thinker Ibn Arabi (1165–1240), who is describing the type of saint closest to God, called a qutb. *What personal and spiritual qualities does such a person exhibit? In what ways are these qualities gendered, that is, linked with generally accepted notions of masculine and feminine qualities? Does al-Sharani seem to be proposing these qualities for all or only for a spiritual elite?*

He is the mirror of the Divine Reality and the locus of the manifestation of the holy attributes, and the master of the moment (*ṣāḥib al-waqt*). He knows the secret of divine determination. He is hidden, because he is preserved in the storehouses of jealousy, wrapped in the garments of fasting. No doubt ever occurs regarding his religion, and no thought occurs to him that contradicts his station. He engages ... in sexual intercourse, ... loving women, giving nature its due within the bounds of the Sharīʿa, and giving the spirit its due within the bounds set by God. ... He is for God alone. His spiritual state is always one of worship and recognizing his need for God. He hates what is evil and approves what is good. He loves the beauty of ornamentation and of persons. The spirits come to him in the best form. He pines away in love, he is jealous for God and angry on His behalf. ... His spirituality appears only behind the veil of the seen and

[1] ahb-DOOL-wah-HAHB.
[2] ahk-MAHD ahl-shah-RAH-nee.

Valerie J. Hoffman, *Sufism, Mystics, and Saints in Modern Egypt* (Columbia: University of South Carolina Press, 1995), 93–94.

ınseen. He sees things only as the locus of the glance of the Di-
'ine. . . . He is persistent in prayer and intercession, unlike those who
are in a spiritual state. The *qutb* is beyond having a spiritual state [of
ecstasy that would make him unmindful of things around him]. He is
fixed in knowledge. . . . He does not transcend spatial limitations or
walk in air or on water. . . . He rarely performs miracles.

23

KATIB CHELEBI

The Balance of Truth

1656

Katib Chelebi[1] *(1609–1657) was a Turkish scholar and minor official in
the Ottoman Empire who wrote more than twenty books on education,
scholarship, religion, geography, and other subjects.* The Balance of
Truth *is a series of brief essays on ideas and practices in Islam that were
controversial in Chelebi's day, as the Ottoman state attempted to enforce a
more uniform Sunni orthodoxy as a result of its conflict with the Safavids.
These include some activities practiced by members of Sufi orders, including spiritual dancing and pilgrimages to holy sites. What is Chelebi's opinion about these activities? What does he think should be done about them?
How might his opinions have been influenced by his position as a government official? As is sometimes the case with religious practices, those who
oppose them provide more detailed and vivid descriptions than those
who support them. How do the Sufi masters who Chelebi quotes defend
spinning as a devotional practice?*

Dancing and Whirling

Now let us come to the motions performed by certain Sufis in the
course of their litany. The orthodox Ulema have classed those

[1]kah-TEEP CHEH-leh-bee.

Katib Chelebi, *The Balance of Truth*, translated by G. L. Lewis (London: George Allen
and Unwin, 1957), 42–45, 92–95.

whirlings as "dancing," and have pronounced it forbidden, branding as infidels those who hold it permissible. The Sufis begin by saying that the definition of dancing is not applicable to it. They continue thus: "The cyclic motion is a form of motion distinct from dancing and for the good of mankind. If it is permitted, there is no harm in it from the point of view of the public good." . . .

If asked what the good of it is, the Sufi reply is as follows. If the adept performs the motions in the ritual, heat is necessarily generated. Thereupon coldness leaves his body, and the vital spirit is spread by the heat all over the body. The spirits and faculties are enlivened and the specific human soul is set in motion too in the measure of his concentration on the performance. Listening to the litany and the music helps in the process too, and the result is a degree of enthusiasm and vigour for motion in the direction of the spiritual world. Many adepts then attain a trance-like state and lose consciousness of the world. The body remains on earth but the soul takes wings towards its own kind. One develops a taste for this condition, as it is said, "Who does not taste does not know." It comes about more quickly with motion than without. By this means, the aspirant advances and soon attains his goal. How can it be denied that physical motion gives motion to spirits and faculties? Young students, when reciting, instinctively move and sway from side to side. For by the motion of the head the brain produces a certain warmth and equilibrium, which lead to an increase in the cogitative power. This fact is noted in some philosophical books.

The answer, not to what the Sufi says but to what he is and does, is this. Most of the Khalwatī Order[2] have based their rites and observances on the community of aspirants. They have founded lodges and have made the *Hay!* and *Hu!* which are the essentials of their vociferation, into the instrument of their society, the pivot of their livelihood, and the prop of their stumbling. Their hypocrisy has turned their ordained music and their obligatory motions, which their ancient founders prescribed for a sound purpose and which ought to be freely permitted to those worthy, into bait for the trap of imposture and a snare for disreputable fools. This is the reason why the brutish common people flock to them, and votive offerings and pious gifts pour into their lodges. Since their gyrations play an important part in this, they will not abandon their spinning. Some fools become spectators, some become disciples and self-styled ascetics. There is no rhyme or

---

[2] *Khalwatī Order*: One of the Sufi orders.

reason to any of it; they falsely extol their sheykhs to the skies and put on an act for the sake of a dinner. They meet together and make their *Hay!* and *Hu!* an instrument of fraud, calling it "Mindfulness of God and Declaration of His Unity." . . .

The orthodox Ulema have interfered with them, as is their duty, writing many tracts against them. . . . The tug-of-war between the two parties has brought them into a vicious circle. At no time has there been a break in the chain of contention; it has grown longer and longer.

The sensible man will neither fall victim to the disease of carping, nor follow their artful designs. . . .

Pilgrimages to Tombs

Former peoples paid great attention and devotion to visiting graves. One account makes this practice the source and origin of the worship of idols. At the beginning of Islam, for this reason, the Glory of the World[3] for a while absolutely forbade visits to tombs, but subsequently allowed them, in these words: 'I had forbidden you to visit tombs, but now you may visit them.' Visiting tombs and addressing supplications to the dead then became lawful.

The point now at issue is the practice of appealing to the dead for help, and on this the Ulema have disagreed. Sheykhs[4] have allowed it, saying, "When you are perplexed, seek help from those in the grave." They have said too, "Inasmuch as the soul is attached to the body, it is also not without attachment to the grave. In the tombs of the great there is a vestige of spirituality. Seeking access to God in such places is preferable to prayer and appeal anywhere else. Has it escaped notice that certain of the great Naqshibendī[5] sheykhs have frequented the tombs of their predecessors and so have borrowed of their spirituality and have taken the Way?"

But most lawyers have said, "To allow the asking of aid from the dead is to slacken the reins of the common people. From this arose idolatry in olden time. First they sought to approach God through the spirits of prophets and saints. Gradually they began to make images of them and to worship them, saying that they were their intercessors with God. It is with this intention that tomb worshippers frequent graves for fasting and prayer." Hence they have absolutely forbidden

[3] *Glory of the World*: The Prophet Muhammad.
[4] That is, Sufi sheikhs.
[5] *Naqshibendī*: One of the Sufi orders.

asking help from the dead. And indeed, they say, this practice is rank polytheism. . . . [But] so long as there is no intention of worshipping the intermediary, no polytheism is involved. . . .

In this way a balance is struck between the extremes of the two factions; on the one hand the people are not absolutely forbidden to visit tombs, on the other the reins are not slackened by giving the common folk absolute licence to ask help from the graves.

And yet it is a fact that among mankind generally lamps are placed in graveyards and that women and children and men of weak intellect have made it their habit to go to graveyards and rub their faces and eyes on the tombs and to anoint themselves with the lamp-oil. This they will not abandon. Caretakers of graveyards and sellers of lamps make their living thereby.

To quarrel and argue with people about this is stupid and futile. They will not be deterred.

24

MOSES CORDOVERO

The Palm Tree of Deborah

1560s

Moses Cordovero[1] *was a leader in the mystical community of Safed in Palestine. He wrote extensively, including long works for highly trained scholars and shorter guides to Kabbalistic ideas and practices for lay-people.* The Palm Tree of Deborah *was one of these brief books of mystical ethics, showing readers how they could imitate God by following the principles of the various* sefirot,[2] *the qualities of the Divine that were at the heart of Kabbalistic teachings. What types of behavior does Cordovero prescribe for those who wish to follow the Kabbalah?*

[1] cohr-doh-VEHR-oh.
[2] seh-fee-ROTE.

Daniel C. Matt, *The Essential Kaballah: The Heart of Jewish Mysticism* (San Francisco: HarperCollins, 1995), 83–85, 88.

Imitate your Creator. Then you will enter the mystery of the supernal form, the divine image in which you were created. If you resemble the divine in body but not in action, you distort the form. People will say of you: "A lovely form whose deeds are ugly." For the essence of the divine image is action. What good is it if your anatomy corresponds to the supernal form, while your actions do not resemble God's? So imitate the acts of Keter,[3] the thirteen qualities of compassion alluded to by the prophet Micah: "Who is a God like you, delighting in love? You will again have compassion upon us. You will hurl all our sins into the depths of the sea."

You should desire the well-being of your fellow creature, eying his good fortune benevolently. Let his honor be as precious to you as your own, for you and your fellow are one and the same. That is why we are commanded: "Love your neighbor as yourself." You should desire what is right for your fellow; never denigrate him or wish for his disgrace. Just as God desires neither our disgrace nor our suffering, because of our close relationship with him, so you should not desire someone else's disgrace, suffering, or ruin. You should feel as bad for such suffering as if it were your own. Similarly, rejoice over another's good fortune as if you were basking in it.

God does not behave as a human being normally behaves. If one person angers another, even after they are reconciled the latter cannot bring himself to love the one who offended him as he loved him before. Yet if you sin and then return to God, your status is higher. As the saying goes, "Those who return to God occupy a place where even the completely righteous cannot stand." So when you return to God, and God restores the divine presence to you, his love for you is not the same as before but all the greater. This is the meaning of: "You will again have compassion upon us." God will increase his compassion, mending us, bringing us closer.

This is how you should behave toward your fellow human being. Do not bear a grudge from the anger you felt. When you see that he wants to make up, be much more compassionate and loving than before. Say to yourself: "He is like one of those who return to God, unrivaled by even the completely righteous." Cultivate a more intimate relationship with him than with those who have been completely righteous with you, who have never offended you.

---

[3] *Keter*: Total compassion, the highest of the *sefirot*.

These are some of the qualities by which you resemble your Creator. The sublime qualities of compassion have a precious characteristic: just as you conduct yourself below, so are you worthy of opening the corresponding sublime quality above. Exactly as you behave, so it emanates from above. You cause that quality to shine in the world.

The quality of humility includes all qualities, since it pertains to Keter. Although Keter transcends all the other qualities, it does not exalt itself; on the contrary, it descends, constantly gazing below. Its emanator constantly gazes into it, bestowing goodness, while it gazes at those beneath.

God nourishes everything, from the horned buffalo to nits, disdaining no creature—for if he disdained creatures due to their insignificance, they could not endure for even a moment. Rather, he gazes and emanates compassion upon them all. So should you be good to all creatures, disdaining none. Even the most insignificant creature should assume importance in your eyes; attend to it. Do good to whomever needs your goodness. . . .

Your ears should always be tuned to hear the good, while rumors and gossip should never be let in, according to the secret of sublime listening. There, no harsh shouting enters, no tongue of evil leaves a blemish. So listen only to positive, useful things, not to things that provoke anger.

Your eyes should not gaze at anything disgraceful. Rather, they should always be open to notice those who suffer, to be compassionate toward them as much as possible. When you see a poor person suffering, do not close your eyes in the slightest. On the contrary, keep him in mind as much as you can; arouse compassion for him—from God and from people.

Your face should always be shining. Welcome each person with a friendly countenance. For with regard to Keter . . ., the supernal crown, it is said: "In the light of the king's face is life." No redness or harsh judgment gains entrance there. So, too, the light of your face should never change; whoever looks at you will find only joy and a friendly expression. Nothing should disturb you.

Your mouth should produce nothing but good. The words you speak should be Torah and an expression of goodwill. Never generate angry or ugly words, curses, or nonsense. Let your mouth resemble the upper mouth, which is never closed, never silent, never withholding the good. Speak positively, always with benevolent words.

25

ISAAC LURIA

Bringing Forth Sparks
1570

In contrast to Cordovero, Isaac Luria,[1] the most influential Kabbalist of the period, wrote very little, commenting that it was impossible to write things down because everything was interrelated and he could never express it all. His teachings, including this brief instruction, were recorded by his pupils and disciples. Luria taught that from God's transcendence emanated a ray of light, which ultimately shattered. Most of the light returned to the Divine Infinite, but some remained imprisoned in the material world as sparks. The goal of human existence is to raise these sparks, restoring them to the Divinity and thus repairing the universe; this is accomplished by living a holy life and understanding that all actions are ethical activities. In this instruction, how does Luria highlight the possibilities for holiness in mundane everyday activities?

You can mend the cosmos by anything you do—even eating. Do not imagine that God wants you to eat for mere pleasure or to fill your belly. No, the purpose is mending.

Sparks of holiness intermingle with everything in the world, even inanimate objects. By saying a blessing before you enjoy something, your soul partakes spiritually. This is food for the soul. As the Torah states: "One does not live on bread alone, but rather on all that issues from the mouth of God." Not just the physical, but the spiritual—the holy sparks, springing from the mouth of God. Like the soul herself, breathed into us by God.

So when you are about to eat bread, say the *motsi*: "Blessed are you, YHVH[2] our God, sovereign of the world, who brings forth bread from the earth." Then by eating, you bring forth sparks that cleave to your soul.

[1] LOO-ree-ah.
[2] *YHVH*: Yahweh, the name of God in Hebrew.

Daniel C. Matt, *The Essential Kaballah: The Heart of Jewish Mysticism* (San Francisco: HarperCollins, 1995), 149.

26

The Pious Customs of Abraham Galante
published 1580s

Abraham Galante (d. 1560) was a follower of Moses Cordovero who wrote commentaries on the Kabbalah and rules of behavior for those living in Safed. The following is a segment of one of these lists of rules. Some of the devotional rituals it describes, such as welcoming the Sabbath with special readings, later became widely followed among Jews living in the Near East and Europe. What religious practices does it prescribe? How does it envision the ideal believer? The town of Safed was in territory ruled by Muslims. What attitude toward secular political authorities emerges here?

---

1. On the eve of the New Moon all the people fast, including men, women, and students. And there is a place where they assemble on that day and remain the entire time, reciting penitential prayers, petitionary devotions, confession of sins, and practicing flagellation. . . .

2. On the night of the New Moon there are men of action who rise at midnight and recite psalms. . . .

8. On the eve of the Feast of Weeks there are those who sleep one or two hours after completely preparing for the festival. This is because, at night, following the [festive] meal, every congregation assembles in its own synagogue and those present do not sleep the whole night long. They read selected portions from the Torah, Prophets, and Hagiographa,[1] the Mishnah,[2] *Zohar*,[3] and rabbinic homilies until the break of dawn. . . .

9. Every Sabbath eve they go out into the field or to the courtyard of the synagogue and welcome the Sabbath. Everyone dresses in his Sabbath garments. They recite the psalm, "Give to the Lord, O heavenly beings" [Ps. 29] and the Sabbath hymn, followed by the "Psalm for the Sabbath day" [Ps. 92]. . . .

[1]*Hagiographa*: Final section of the Hebrew Bible.
[2]*Mishnah*: Works of Jewish law.
[3]*Zohar*: Group of mystical works, the most important texts in Kabbalah.

Lawrence Fine, ed., *Judaism in Practice from the Middle Ages through the Early Modern Period* (Princeton, N.J.: Princeton University Press, 2001), 379–82.

16. On the eve of the three pilgrimage festivals [Passover, Feast of Weeks, Sukkot] there are men of good deeds who purchase a lamb and divide it among the poor. . . .

18. The pious are careful to pray with the congregation in the evening, morning, and afternoon.

19. One ought to be among the first ten persons at the synagogue for worship in the morning as well as in the evening.

20. It is proper to avoid conversation during the entire prayer service, as well as while the Torah scroll is open. This prohibition even includes conversation having to do with matters of Torah.

21. It is proper to establish regular times for the study of Torah, during the daytime as well as at night, and to refrain from sleeping before periods of study. . . .

23. An individual ought to forgive transgressions and to pardon anyone who injures him, whether through speech or deed. It is all the more important never to take such a person to a [non-Jewish] court, where they employ idolatrous practices.

24. A person should wash his hands when he rises from bed before touching anything whatsoever and before treading upon the ground. This is in order to drive away impure spirits.

25. When an individual leaves his house, it is fitting for him to place his hand upon the *mezuzah* [on the doorpost] so as to remind himself of God's unity and of His commandments. . . .

27. There are certain especially pious individuals who fulfill the tithe obligation [to the poor] by doubling it, that is, with one-fifth of all their earnings. They set aside their money in a chest so that they have it available to them and can give generously in fulfillment of their pledge. Even among the poor themselves there are those who follow this custom.

4

South Asia: Syncretism and Sikhism in the Mughal Empire

BACKGROUND

At about the time the Ottomans and Safavids were battling each other, another Muslim ruler was expanding his holdings. In the 1520s the ruler of Central Asia, Zahir al-Din Muhammad Babur (1483–1530), conquered northwestern India, where adherents of many religious traditions lived. The empire he established was called the "Mughal,"[1] from the Persian word for Mongol, for Babur claimed to be descended from the famous Mongol warriors Chinggis Khan and Timur. Babur's son Humayun lost the empire to the Afghan sultan Sher Shah, but regained it with the aid of troops from the Safavid Empire. Humayun died in an accident shortly after returning to power, and his son Akbar (whose name means "greater than anything else") took over the throne in 1556, when he was only thirteen. Akbar was a brilliant military leader, and his empire grew to cover two-thirds of South Asia, including most of present-day Afghanistan, Pakistan, north and central India, and Bangladesh.

Babur and Humayun were Sunni Muslims, but both were forced to convert to Shi'a Islam in order to obtain Safavid military aid. Humayun appointed a Shi'a noble as regent for his young son, which angered the Sunni *ulama*, the body of legal scholars at the Mughal court. Akbar's deviations from Sunni Islam went far beyond those of his father, however. He appointed both Sunnis and Shi'as as officials, and also appointed Hindus, the religion of most of the population of the Mughal Empire. *Hinduism* is the name given later, when this area was a British colony, to the very old and very diverse religious traditions of India. Hindus varied (and continue to vary) in their forms of worship, beliefs about the gods and goddesses, festivals, texts, saints, rituals,

[1] MOO-guhl.

and shrines, though they shared a group of sacred writings and a belief in reincarnation. At the time of the expansion of the Mughal Empire, many Hindus were followers of *bhakti*, a devotional movement that emphasized personal love of one particular manifestation of the divine. *Bhakti* teachers downplayed caste divisions, asserting that all believers could be spiritually worthy. Many *bhakti* teachers were mystics, and the movement had much in common with Sufism in Islam, for both emphasized close emotional relations between the individual and God more than specific doctrines or rituals. In fact, in the same way that some holy places in the Ottoman Empire were shared by Christians and Muslims, some individuals were revered as saints by both Sufi brotherhoods and *bhakti* groups, and their writings, usually in the form of mystical poetry, are a common heritage of northern India.

Akbar won support from Hindu leaders, especially the powerful Rajputs, a group of nobles who had previously ruled much of northern India, by making them administrators and military commanders. He cemented these alliances through marriage, marrying several princesses from Rajput families himself and encouraging other Mughal nobles to marry Hindu princesses. He let his Hindu subjects continue to follow Hindu law and custom and further enhanced support for his rule by ending the special tax on non-Muslims collected in most states ruled by Islamic law, thus moving in exactly the opposite direction from that advocated by al-Maghili in northern Africa. (See Chapter 3, Document 19.)

Akbar's toleration of religious differences was not motivated simply by the practical concerns of ruling, however, for he thought that bringing religions together would promote justice and harmony. To that end, in 1575 he built the *Ibadat Khana* (House of Worship), where scholars from various religions could discuss their beliefs and practices in front of the emperor. These discussions, illustrated on the cover of this book and in Document 29, involved both Sunni and Shi'a Muslims and also included representatives from other religious traditions followed in the Mughal Empire. There were Zoroastrians, followers of an ancient Persian religious leader named Zoroaster, who taught that the world is a battle between the forces of good and the forces of evil. Indian Zoroastrians were called Parsis (which means "Persians" in Hindi, one of the languages spoken in India) and believed that each person would be judged on how well he or she had stood up for the forces of good. There were Jains, a religion founded in India in the 500s BCE, who believed (and continue to believe) that all life is sacred because every physical body contains an eternal soul.

There were atheists of the Carvaka tradition, who believed that the world was simply material and did not involve divine forces. There were Indian Christians from the southwest coast of India, usually termed the *Malabar Christians*, whose church dated back to the fifth century and may have been even older. There were Jesuit priests from the Portuguese colony of Goa on the west coast of India. There were Sikhs, a new religion founded by Guru Nanak during Babur's reign (Guru Nanak is discussed in more detail below). (See Documents 27 and 28.)

Many members of the Sunni *ulama* were suspicious of these discussions, but in 1579 a number of them agreed that Akbar would be the final arbiter in religious disputes over issues for which there was no clear written tradition. In 1582 Akbar went further, establishing what he termed the "Divine Faith" (*Din-i-Ilahi*) that combined ideas and rituals from many religions. (See Document 30.) The Divine Faith also included ceremonies showing respect for Akbar, for Akbar clearly saw himself as the center of this new religion. Loyalty to the emperor, he thought, along with shared religious ideas, would unite India's many religious and ethnic groups. Many of his courtiers supported him in this, capturing it in the phrase "Allahu Akbar," which, because of the meaning of "Akbar," means both "God is greater than anything else" and "God is Akbar." More traditional Muslim scholars were horrified at this phrase, seeing it as emperor worship, which is strictly forbidden in Islam.

This new Divine Faith did not spread beyond the court, nor last much beyond Akbar's death. His great-grandson Dara Shikoh (1615–1659) showed similar interests in multiple religious traditions and spiritual unity, but he was killed by his brother Aurangzeb (1618–1707), who favored a stricter adherence to Sunni Islam. For a combination of religious, political, and economic reasons, Aurangzeb undid many of the measures of toleration taken by Akbar. The Mughal Empire reached its largest size under Aurangzeb's rule, but his policies alienated many of his subjects and there were rebellions by Hindu and Sikh groups.

The multiple religious traditions found in northern India encouraged many other thinkers along with Akbar to develop their own devotional systems that blended existing elements in new ways. The most important of these was Guru Nanak, a religious teacher who lived in the Punjab area of what is now the India-Pakistan border. In contrast to Akbar's short-lived Divine Faith, the religion based on Guru Nanak's teachings, Sikhism, spread widely and today is found around the world.

Nanak was born into a relatively high-caste Hindu family in an area ruled by a Muslim governor. He received a good education, became a storekeeper, married, and had several children. During this relatively uneventful period of his life, he also listened to the ideas of a number of teachers, including Sufi and *bhakti* mystics. Around 1500, he left his family and city, and began traveling through many parts of India and perhaps beyond. Living as a wandering ascetic, he traveled with a low-status Muslim musician named Mardana, and came to believe that everyone has equal status in the eyes of God. His writings indicate that he saw some of the fighting that occurred as part of Babur's establishment of the Mughal Empire in the 1520s, and about this time he established a new village for his followers, Kartarpur, on the banks of the Ravi River in the Punjab. His family rejoined him, and he lived the rest of his life there as the head of a household and of a growing community of followers that gathered around him.

About the time that he first left his home, Nanak began to develop his own religious ideas, which centered on the absolute unity and majesty of God. God is—in words often repeated in Nanak's writings—unseen, infinite, formless, ineffable, and eternal. God is unknowable in totality but also knowable to a limited degree through God's creation. People can come to know God through meditation on manifestations of the divine presence in the world, and particularly through looking inward, for God is also present in the human heart. Salvation can come once one recognizes complete dependency on God, who bestows unmerited grace on unworthy sinners through revelation. Before they come to God, according to Nanak, people often concentrate on worldly values such as money or fame. Such things are not evil in and of themselves, but they are unreality (*maya*), an illusion or deception that keeps one from realizing that God alone exists; concern with worldly values keeps one separate from God. Religious devotions such as specific prayers, pilgrimages, or rituals might also entangle people in *maya* if they viewed these external observances themselves as worthy and did not concentrate on their inward meaning and purpose. This criticism of empty ritual was very similar to those Erasmus and Luther were making at exactly the same time in Europe. Nanak emphasized that proper devotional discipline could be done by people living in families and involved with the ordinary things of the world. In fact, service to others was an important part of spiritual life, and living in the world with a family was spiritually superior to renouncing family ties.

Turning away from *maya* to God is difficult for humans to do alone, and in this they often need a teacher, or *guru*. In Nanak's writings, the word *guru* usually means the voice of God itself, akin to the Holy Spirit in Christian theology. This was experienced inwardly, and directed the believer to develop a devotional discipline often described as *nam simran*, or remembrance of the Divine Name. Through *nam simran*, believers can come to recognize the Divine Order of the universe and attempt to bring themselves into harmony with this. Nanak viewed this as a gradual process of ascending stages of increasing unity with God. The final stage brought one out of the endless chain of reincarnation and transmigration of souls in which one is repeatedly separated from God.

Nanak named one of his followers as his successor, beginning a line of leadership that lasted into the early eighteenth century. Gradually the word *guru* came to be applied to this series of men, who built on the teachings of Nanak and transformed the followers of his teachings into a community that adopted the name *Sikh*, which means "learner." His followers spread the Sikh message, and both Hindus and Muslims converted, though converts included significantly more Hindus. The third Sikh guru, Amar Das (guruship 1552–1574), set up a system for overseeing believers and local leaders and developed rituals and ceremonies for major life changes, including birth, marriage, and death. The fourth guru, Ram Das (guruship 1574–1581), founded the city of Amritsar, and the fifth guru, Arjan Dev (guruship 1581–1606) constructed a major temple, the Harimandir Sahib (Temple of God), which became the holiest place in the Sikh world. (In the nineteenth century, the temple was covered in gold, and marble decorations were added, so it is often referred to as the Golden Temple.) Arjan Dev also compiled a collection of Sikh sacred writings, the *Adi Granth* ("first book"), which consists primarily of hymns and prayers written by the gurus to direct believers in their devotions. (See Documents 31–33.)

The *Adi Granth* contains the writings of Nanak, written in Punjabi, a language spoken in northwestern India, rather than in Sanskrit, the language of the ancient Hindu texts. Like the Protestant reformers who were preaching in Germany at the same time, Nanak thought it was important that people who were not members of the educated elite have access to religious writings.

During Nanak's lifetime and those of the second and third gurus, the Sikh community was too small to be viewed with much concern by local Muslim authorities, who regarded Sikhs as simply yet another variety of Hindus or as one of the many movements that blended various traditions common in northern India. Akbar, in fact, admired the

Sikh gurus and invited Sikh representatives to his Hall of Worship. By the early seventeenth century this had changed, and intense conflict with Mughal authorities often erupted. Most later Sikh gurus were military as well as spiritual leaders, but they continued to emphasize that external practices without inner devotion are useless *maya*.

Sikhs thus shared certain aspects of belief with the followers of other religions in India: Like Hindus, they believed in reincarnation; like Muslims, they rejected the use of religious images and emphasized the absolute oneness of God; like Zoroastrians, they taught that believers should actively resist evil rather than concentrate only on the next life. For Sikhs, however, their most important ideas come directly from God through Nanak's revelations.

DOCUMENTS

The many religious traditions in South Asia produced written and visual sources of all types. For the developments at Akbar's court, though, the emperor left no writings of his own. However, his chief adviser and close friend Abu'l Fazl more than filled the gap, leaving a huge history of Akbar's reign, the *Akbarnama*. In the *Akbarnama*, Abu'l Fazl includes speeches given by Akbar, though there is no way of knowing whether or not the emperor actually made these speeches. Similar speeches appear in writings of other authors, however, including Muslim historians hostile to Akbar, Portuguese priests who hoped to convert him to Christianity, and Zoroastrian authors interested in his religious policies. The fact that authors with such different points of view all report much the same information indicates that Akbar's ideas and words may be quite accurately represented in these sources. In fact, this is the same way that Luther's lectures have been preserved—they were also recorded by others, and variant versions later compared and published, though we have no way of knowing if they were exactly what he said.

The writings of Guru Nanak and the other early gurus were compiled into the *Adi Granth* by the fifth guru, Arjan Dev, at the end of the sixteenth century. They were increasingly regarded as sacred, a status that was enhanced when the tenth guru, Guru Gobind Singh, declared that the book itself, which he expanded slightly into the longer *Guru Granth*, was to be regarded as a living guru. The *Guru Granth* primarily consists of a series of *Bani*, sets of verses composed by one of the ten Sikh gurus, with certain passages to be recited or read every day by devout Sikhs. It also includes writings by Hindu and Muslim poets and teachers who lived in the twelfth through the sixteenth centuries and whose ideas fit with Sikh teachings on the importance of inner knowledge of God.

In analyzing the documents in this chapter, you will see that those about Akbar (see Documents 27–30) cover the same developments, but have very different opinions about them and about Akbar himself, ranging from hostile to flattering. How does the author's own religious allegiance shape his point of view? Why is it important to have a range of sources? What can historians gain from using hostile sources? How do the various authors portray the interactions at Akbar's court and the relationship between Akbar's political and religious roles? Turning to other themes of this book, how is God's power portrayed in the Sikh texts (see Documents 31–33), and how does Akbar describe it (see Document 27)? How is human ability to comprehend that power portrayed? How would you compare the statement of basic beliefs in Akbar's Divine Faith (see Document 30) with that of Guru Nanak (see Document 31)? What do the Sikh texts set out as basic duties of the believer, and how are these different for men and women? (For questions that relate these sources to those in other chapters in the book, see p. 163.)

27

ABU'L FAZL

Akbarnama

ca. 1590

Abu'l Fazl[1] (1551–1602) came from a family of Sunni Muslim scholars and poets, but, like Akbar himself, was interested in a wide variety of religious ideas. Over many years, Abu'l Fazl composed the Akbarnama,[2] *an enormous history of Akbar's reign and those of his predecessors. In the*

[1] AHB-uhl FAHZ-uhl.
[2] ak-bar-NAH-ma.

The Akbarnama of Abu-l-Fazl, translated by Henry Beveridge (Delhi: Rare Books, 1939), 3:158, 160, 364–71.

following sections, he talks about Akbar's establishment of the House of Worship and describes the discussions that occurred there. Abu'l Fazl was assassinated on the order of Akbar's son, the later Emperor Jahangir, who was in revolt against his father at the time. What is Abu'l Fazl's attitude toward Akbar? Toward the Sunni Muslim ulama? What does he see as the appropriate role for a ruler in religious life?

At this time[3] when the capital . . . was illuminated by his glorious advent, H.M.[4] ordered that a house of worship should be built in order to the adornment of the spiritual kingdom, and that it should have four verandahs. . . .

A general proclamation was issued that, on that night of illumination, all orders and sects of mankind—those who searched after spiritual and physical truth, and those of the common public who sought for an awakening, and the inquirers of every sect—should assemble in the precincts of the holy edifice, and bring forward their spiritual experiences, and their degrees of knowledge of the truth in various and contradictory forms in the bridal chamber of manifestation.

Wisdom and deeds would be tested, and the essence of manhood would be exhibited. . . .

A set of wisdom-loving, judicious men were in readiness to propound questions and to record views. The difficulties of the various classes of men were fittingly resolved. The mirrors of the inquirers of the Age were polished. The whole of that night was kept alive by discussions which approved themselves to one and all. The degrees of reason and the stages of vision were tested, and all the heights and depths of intelligence were traversed, and the lamp of perception was brightened. By the blessedness of the holy examination, the real was separated from the fictitious, and the uncurrency of those who were only coated with wisdom was brought to light. . . .

It has been mentioned that he, in his ample search after truth, had laid the foundation of a noble seat for intellectual meetings. His sole and sublime idea was that . . . the masters of science and ethics, and the devotees of piety and contemplation, be tested, the principles of faiths and creeds be examined, religions be investigated, the proofs and evidences for each be considered, and the pure gold and the alloy

[3] 1575.
[4] *H.M.*: His Majesty, i.e., Akbar.

be separated from evil commixture. In a short space of time a beautiful, detached building was erected, and the fraudulent vendors of impostures put to sleep in the privy chamber of contempt. A noble palace was provided for the spiritual world, and the pillars of Divine knowledge rose high. . . .

Ṣūfī, philosopher, orator, jurist, Sunnī, S̲h̲īa, Brahman, Jatī,[5] Sīūrā,[6] Cārbāk,[7] Nazarene,[8] Jew, Ṣābī,[9] Zoroastrian, and others enjoyed exquisite pleasure by beholding the calmness of the assembly, the sitting of the world-lord in the lofty pulpit, and the adornment of the pleasant abode of impartiality. The treasures of secrets were opened out without fear of hostile seekers after battle. The just and truth-perceiving ones of each sect emerged from haughtiness and conceit, and began their search anew. They displayed profundity and meditation, and gathered eternal bliss on the divan of greatness. The conceited and quarrelsome from evilness of disposition and shortness of thought descended into the mire of presumption and sought their profit in loss. . . .

The bigoted 'Ulamā and the routine-lawyers, who reckoned themselves among the chiefs of philosophies and leaders of enlightenment, found their position difficult. . . . They recognized wisdom nowhere but in the schools, and did not know that acquired knowledge is for the most part stained with doubts and suspicions. Insight is that which without schooling illuminates the pure temple of the heart. The inner soul receives rays from holy heaven. . . .

Continually, in those day-like nights, glorious subtleties and profound words dropped from his [Akbar's] pearl-filled mouth. Among them was this: "Most persons, from intimacy with those who adorn their outside, but are inwardly bad, think that outward semblance, and the letter of Muhammadanism, profit without internal conviction. Hence we by fear and force compelled many believers in the Brahman [i.e., Hindu] religion to adopt the faith of our ancestors. Now that the light of truth has taken possession of our soul, it has become clear that in this distressful place of contrarities (the world), where darkness of comprehension and conceit are heaped up, fold upon fold, a single step cannot be taken without the torch of proof, and that that creed is profitable

---

[5] *Jatī*: Jain ascetic.
[6] *Sīūrā*: Jain.
[7] *Cārbāk*: Carvaka atheist.
[8] *Nazarene*: Western Christian.
[9] *Ṣābī*: Malabar Christian.

which is adopted with the approval of wisdom. To repeat the creed, to remove a piece of skin [i.e., to become circumcised] and to place the end of one's bones on the ground[10] from dread of the Sultan, is not seeking after God." . . .

He also said, "We blame ourselves for what we did in accordance with old rules and before the truth about faith had shed its rays on our heart."

The fortunate and suspicious, on hearing these enlightening words, hastened to the abode of the light of search and set themselves to amend their ways, while the somnolent and perverse were full of disturbance. Inasmuch as the fierce winds of indiscrimination had laid hold of the four corners of the world, he mentioned the rules of various religions, and described their various excellencies. The acute sovereign gave no weight to common talk, and praised whatever was good in any religion. He often adorned the tablet of his tongue by saying "He is a man who makes Justice the guide of the path of inquiry, and takes from every sect what is consonant to reason."

[10]*to place the end of one's bones on the ground*: To touch one's head to the ground.

28

'ABD UL-QADIR BADA'UNI

Selected Histories

ca. 1590

'Abd ul-Qadir Bada'uni[1] *(1540–ca. 1615) was an orthodox Sunni Muslim historian who also described the scene at the Hall of Worship. In much of his history, including the first section here, Bada'uni asserts that Akbar wanted to destroy Islam in India, but most historians view this as an overstatement. Akbar did celebrate non-Islamic festivals, but he was being eclectic, and he continued in his Muslim practices as well. What is*

[1]ahb-DOOLKAH-deer bah-dah-OO-nee.

Wm. Theodore de Bary et al., eds., *Sources of Indian Tradition* (New York: Columbia University Press, 1958), 439–41.

Bada'uni's opinion about Akbar's attempts at religious blending? What is his attitude toward other religious traditions and toward types of Islam that differ from his Sunni orthodoxy?

In the year nine hundred and eighty-three the buildings of the House of Worship were completed. The cause was this. For many years previously the emperor had gained in succession remarkable and decisive victories. The empire had grown in extent from day to day; everything turned out well, and no opponent was left in the whole world. His Majesty had thus leisure to come into nearer contact with ascetics and the disciples of his reverence [the late] Mu'īn, and passed much of his time in discussing the Word of God and the word of the Prophet. Questions of Sufism, scientific discussions, inquiries into philosophy and law, were the order of the day. . . .

And later that day the emperor came to Fathpūr. There he used to spend much time in the Hall of Worship in the company of learned men and shaikhs and especially on Friday nights, when he would sit up there the whole night continually occupied in discussing questions of religion, whether fundamental or collateral. The learned men used to draw the sword of the tongue on the battlefield of mutual contradiction and opposition, and the antagonism of the sects reached such a pitch that they would call one another fools and heretics. The controversies used to pass beyond the differences of Sunni, and Shī'a, . . . of lawyer and divine, and they would attack the very bases of belief. And Makhdum-ul-Mulk wrote a treatise to the effect that Shaikh 'Abd-al-Nabī had unjustly killed Khizr Khān Sarwānī, who had been suspected of blaspheming the Prophet [peace be upon him!], and Mīr Habsh, who had been suspected of being a Shī'a, and saying that it was not right to repeat the prayers after him, because he was undutiful toward his father, and was himself afflicted with hemorrhoids. Shaikh 'Abd-al-Nabī replied to him that he was a fool and a heretic. Then the mullās [Muslim theologians] became divided into two parties, and one party took one side and one the other, and became very Jews and Egyptians for hatred of each other. And persons of novel and whimsical opinions, in accordance with their pernicious ideas and vain doubts, coming out of ambush, decked the false in the garb of the true, and wrong in the dress of right, and cast the emperor, who was possessed of an excellent disposition, and was an earnest searcher after truth, but very ignorant and a mere tyro, and used to the company of infidels and base persons, into perplexity, till doubt was heaped upon doubt, and he lost all definite aim, and the straight wall of the clear law and of firm religion was broken down, so that after five or six years not a trace of Islam was left in him: and everything was turned topsy-turvy. . . .

And Samanas [Hindu or Buddhist ascetics] and Brahmans (who as far as the matter of private interviews is concerned gained the advantage over every one in attaining the honor of interviews with His Majesty, and in associating with him, and were in every way superior in reputation to all learned and trained men for their treatises on morals, and on physical and religious sciences, and in religious ecstasies, and stages of spiritual progress and human perfections) brought forward proofs, based on reason and traditional testimony, for the truth of their own, and the fallacy of our religion, and inculcated their doctrine with such firmness and assurance that they affirmed mere imaginations as though they were self-evident facts, the truth of which the doubts of the sceptic could no more shake "Than the mountains crumble, and the heavens be cleft!" And the Resurrection, and Judgment, and other details and traditions, of which the Prophet was the repository, he laid all aside. And he made his courtiers continually listen to those revilings and attacks against our pure and easy, bright and holy faith. . . .

Some time before this a Brahman, named Puruk'hotam, who had written a commentary on the Book, *Increase of Wisdom* (*Khirad-afzā*), had had private interviews with him, and he had asked him to invent particular Sanskrit names for all things in existence. And at one time a Brahman named Debi, who was one of the interpreters of the *Mahābhārata*, was pulled up the wall of the castle sitting on a bedstead till he arrived near a balcony, which the emperor had made his bed-chamber. Whilst thus suspended he instructed His Majesty in the secrets and legends of Hinduism in the manner of worshiping idols, the fire, the sun and stars, and of revering the chief gods of these unbelievers, such as Brahma, Mahadev [Shiva], Bishn [Vishnu], Kishn [Krishna], Ram, and Mahama (whose existence as sons of the human race is a supposition, but whose nonexistence is a certainty, though in their idle belief they look on some of them as gods, and some as angels). His Majesty, on hearing further how much the people of the country prized their institutions, began to look upon them with affection. . . .

Sometimes again it was Shaikh Tāj ud-dīn whom he sent for. This shaikh was son of Shaikh Zakarīya of Ajodhan. . . . He had been a pupil of Rashīd Shaikh Zamān of Panipat, author of a commentary on the *Paths* (*Lawā'ih*), and of other excellent works, was most excellent in Sufism, and in the knowledge of theology second only to Shaikh Ibn

'Arabī and had written a comprehensive commentary on the *Joy of the Souls* (*Nuzhat ul-Arwāh*). Like the preceding he was drawn up the wall of the castle in a blanket, and His Majesty listened the whole night to his Sufic obscenities and follies. The shaikh, since he did not in any great degree feel himself bound by the injunctions of the law, introduced arguments concerning the unity of existence, such as idle Sufis discuss, and which eventually lead to license and open heresy....

Learned monks also from Europe, who are called *Padre*, and have an infallible head, called *Papa*, who is able to change religious ordinances as he may deem advisable for the moment, and to whose authority kings must submit, brought the Gospel, and advanced proofs for the Trinity. His Majesty firmly believed in the truth of the Christian religion, and wishing to spread the doctrines of Jesus, ordered Prince Murād[2] to take a few lessons in Christianity under good auspices, and charged Abū'l Fazl to translate the Gospel....

Fire worshipers also came from Nousarī in Gujarat, proclaimed the religion of Zardusht [Zarathustra] as the true one, and declared reverence to fire to be superior to every other kind of worship. They also attracted the emperor's regard, and taught him the peculiar terms, the ordinances, the rites and ceremonies of the Kaianians [a pre-Muslim Persian dynasty]. At last he ordered that the sacred fire should be made over to the charge of Abū'l Fazl, and that after the manner of the kings of Persia, in whose temples blazed perpetual fires, he should take care it was never extinguished night or day, for that it is one of the signs of God, and one light from His lights....

His Majesty also called some of the yogis, and gave them at night private interviews, inquiring into abstract truths; their articles of faith; their occupation; the influence of pensiveness; their several practices and usages; the power of being absent from the body; or into alchemy, physiognomy, and the power of omnipresence of the soul.

---

[2]*Prince Murād*: Akbar's son.

29

NAN SINGH

Scholars Gather at Akbar's Court
1605

In this illustration from a manuscript of Abu'l Fazl's Akbarnama, *produced in about 1605 by the Sikh artist Nan Singh, Akbar sits on a chair in the middle. The scholars, including Jesuit priests dressed in black on the left, sit on an elaborate carpet with sacred books in front of them as they discuss their points. Outside the walls are beggars holding a food bowl and a groom with horses. Judging by the way Nan Singh shows the various scholars, how would you assess his opinion about the value of different religious traditions? How does he portray the discussions themselves? How would you assess Nan Singh's opinion about Akbar as expressed in his painting?*

120

30

MUHSIN-I-FANI

School of Religion

ca. 1650

Muhsin-i-Fani[1] *(d. 1670?) was a Persian Zoroastrian scholar who wrote about religion at Akbar's court about fifty years after Akbar's death and described Akbar's Divine Faith. Despite the fact that Akbar was the political ruler and had been granted religious authority by the body of Muslim scholars at his court, he never attempted to force his new faith on his subjects through legal, administrative, or military measures. There is no comprehensive statement of faith directly from Akbar similar to those issued by Protestant and Catholic authorities during the course of the Reformation, but this is a relatively clear statement of key ideas and practices. How does Muhsin-i-Fani view Akbar? How does he describe Akbar's understanding of the nature of God? What qualities are believers supposed to embody, and what actions should they do to demonstrate these qualities?*

Know for certain that the perfect prophet and learned apostle, the possessor of fame, Akbar, that is, the lord of wisdom, directs us to acknowledge that the self-existent being is the wisest teacher, and ordains the creatures with absolute power, so that the intelligent among them may be able to understand his precepts; and as reason renders it evident that the world has a Creator, all-mighty and all-wise, who has diffused upon the field of events among the servants, subject to vicissitudes, numerous and various benefits which are worthy of praise and thanksgiving; therefore, according to the lights of our reason, let us investigate the mysteries of his creation, and, according to our knowledge, pour out the praises of his benefits. . . .

In the sequel it became evident to wise men that emancipation is to be obtained only by the knowledge of truth conformably with the precepts of the perfect prophet, the perfect lord of fame, Akbar, "the

[1] MOO-seen-ee-FAH-nee.

Wm. Theodore de Bary et al., eds., *Sources of Indian Tradition* (New York: Columbia University Press, 1958), 443–44.

Wise"; the practices enjoined by him are: renouncing and abandoning the world; refraining from lust, sensuality, entertainment, slaughter of what possesses life; and from appropriating to one's self the riches of other men; abstaining from women, deceit, false accusation, oppression, intimidation, foolishness, and giving [to others] opprobrious titles. The endeavors for the recompense of the other world, and the forms of the true religion may be comprised in ten virtues, namely, 1) liberality and beneficence; 2) forbearance from bad actions and repulsion of anger with mildness; 3) abstinence from worldly desires; 4) care of freedom from the bonds of the worldly existence and violence, as well as accumulating previous stores for the future real and perpetual world; 5) piety, wisdom, and devotion, with frequent meditations on the consequences of actions; 6) strength of dexterous prudence in the desire of sublime actions; 7) soft voice, gentle words, and pleasing speeches for everybody; 8) good society with brothers, so that their will may have the precedence to our own; 9) a perfect alienation from the creatures, and a perfect attachment to the supreme Being; 10) purification of the soul by the yearning after God the all-just, and the union with the merciful Lord, in such a manner that, as long as the soul dwells in the body, it may think itself one with him and long to join him, until the hour of separation from the body arrives.

31

The Japji Sahib[1] from the Guru Granth

The Guru Granth *begins with Guru Nanak's composition entitled "Japji" (which means "respected chant" or "venerated chant"), a poetic work comprised of thirty-eight stanzas and two couplets. The Japji opens with the* Mul Mantar, *an invocation and basic statement of faith. Sikhs are to recite the Japji, or at least part of it, every morning. How are God's power and will depicted here? How are believers to demonstrate their faith? What role do social differences, such as wealth or gender, play in religious life?*

[1] JOP-jee SAH-heeb.

Selections from the Sacred Writings of the Sikhs, translated by Trilochan Singh et al. (New York: Macmillan, 1960), 28–33, 37–40, 47–48.

There is one God,[2]
Eternal Truth is His Name;
Maker of all things,
Fearing nothing and at enmity with nothing,
Timeless is His Image;
Not begotten, being of His own Being:
By the grace of the Guru, made known to men.

Jap: The Meditation

AS HE WAS IN THE BEGINNING: THE TRUTH,
SO THROUGHOUT THE AGES,
HE EVER HAS BEEN: THE TRUTH,
SO EVEN NOW HE IS TRUTH IMMANENT,
SO FOR EVER AND EVER HE SHALL BE
    TRUTH ETERNAL.

1

It is not through thought that He is to be comprehended
Though we strive to grasp Him a hundred thousand times;
Nor by outer silence and long deep meditation
Can the inner silence be reached;
Nor is man's hunger for God appeasable
By piling up world-loads of wealth.
All the innumerable devices of worldly wisdom
Leave a man disappointed; not one avails.

How then shall we know the Truth?
How shall we rend the veils of untruth away?
Abide thou by His Will, and make thine own,
His will, O Nānak, that is written in thy heart.

2

Through His Will He creates all the forms of things,
But what the form of His Will is, who can express?
All life is shaped by His ordering,
By His ordering some are high, some of low estate,
Pleasure and pain are bestowed as His Writ ordaineth.

[2] In the original language, references to God are without gender; English translations generally translate genderless pronouns as masculine.

Some through His Will are graciously rewarded,
Others must grope through births and deaths;
Nothing at all, outside His Will, is abiding.
O Nānak, he who is aware of the Supreme Will
Never in his selfhood utters the boast: "It is I."

5

He cannot be installed like an idol,
Nor can man shape His likeness.
He made Himself and maintains Himself
On His heights unstained for ever;
Honoured are they in His shrine
Who meditate upon Him.

Sing thou, O Nānak, the psalms
Of God as the treasury
Of sublime virtues.
If a man sings of God and hears of Him,
And lets love of God sprout within him,
All sorrow shall depart;
In the soul, God will create abiding peace.

The Word of the Guru is the inner Music;
The Word of the Guru is the highest Scripture;
The Word of the Guru is all pervading,
The Guru is Śiva, the Guru is Vishṇu and Brahma,
The Guru is the Mother goddess.

If I knew Him as He truly is
What words could utter my knowledge?
Enlightened by God, the Guru has unravelled one mystery
"There is but one Truth, one Bestower of life;
May I never forget Him."

6

I would bathe in the holy rivers
If so I could win His love and grace;
But of what use is the pilgrimage
If it pleaseth Him not that way?

What creature obtains anything here
Except through previous good acts?
Yet hearken to the Word of the Guru
And his counsel within thy spirit
Shall shine like precious stone.

The Guru's divine illumination
Has unravelled one mystery;
There is but one Bestower of life
May I forget Him never.

17

There is no counting of men's prayers,
There is no counting their ways of adoration.
Thy lovers, O Lord, are numberless;
Numberless those who read aloud from the Vedas;
Numberless those Yogis who are detached from the world;

Numberless are Thy Saints contemplating,
Thy virtues and Thy wisdom;
Numberless are the benevolent, the lovers of their kind.

Numberless Thy heroes and martyrs
Facing the steel of their enemies;
Numberless those who in silence
Fix their deepest thoughts upon Thee;

How can an insignificant creature like myself
Express the vastness and wonder of Thy creation?
I am too petty to have anything to offer Thee;
I cannot, even once, be a sacrifice unto Thee.
To abide by Thy Will, O Lord, is man's best offering;
Thou who art Eternal, abiding in Thy Peace.

21

Pilgrimages, penances, compassion and almsgiving
Bring a little merit, the size of sesame seed.
But he who hears and believes and loves the Name
Shall bathe and be made clean
In a place of pilgrimage within him.

All goodness is Thine, O Lord, I have none;
Though without performing good deeds
None can aspire to adore Thee.
Blessed Thou the Creator and the Manifestation,
Thou art the word, Thou art the primal Truth and Beauty,
And Thou the heart's joy and desire. . . .

32

Let my tongue become a hundred thousand tongues,
Let the hundred thousand be multiplied twenty-fold,
With each tongue many hundred thousands of times
I would repeat the holy Name of the Lord;
Thus let the soul step by step
Mount the stairs to the Bridegroom
And become one with Him.

On hearing of heavenly things,
He who can only crawl also longs to fly.
By God's grace alone, saith Nānak, is God to be grasped.
All else is false, all else is vanity.

33

Ye have no power to speak or in silence listen,
To ask or to give away;
Ye have no power to live or die,
Ye have no power to acquire wealth and dominion and be vain,
Ye have no power to compel the mind to thought or reason,
He who hath the power, He creates and sees;
O Nānak, before the Lord there is no low or high degree.

32

Hymns of Guru Amar Das

1560s

The Guru Granth *includes thousands of hymns and prayers written by the ten Sikh gurus to direct believers in their devotions. Many of these include specific admonitions about issues facing the Sikh community. The third guru, Amar Das, was concerned that many Sikh converts from Hinduism, of which he was one, were retaining ideas about the importance of caste and Hindu spiritual practices. Some of his verses discuss such practices, including* sati, *a word that originally meant "good wife," and came to be used for a woman who killed herself by climbing on her husband's funeral pyre as his body was being cremated. How does Amar Das regard* sati? *What is his opinion of spiritual practices done without concentration on their inner meaning?*

ix

Knowledge of the Transcendent is not to be obtained,
Through outward religious observances, without knowledge,
Doubt and delusion will not depart;
No amount of outward observances
Will remove doubt and delusion.
The mind is filthy with ignorance,
How can it be made clean?
Wash thy mind, O man, in the light of the Word,
And fix thy heart and thy soul upon the Lord.
Saith Nānak: It is by the grace of the Guru
That knowledge of the Transcendent is obtained.
In this way only will doubt and delusion depart.

Selections from the Sacred Writings of the Sikhs, translated by Trilochan Singh et al. (New York: Macmillan, 1960), 129–30, 135, 136.

x

Those who, impure within, seem pure outwardly,
Fair without and foul within, have gambled their lives away,
They have contracted the vile disease of desire;
They have forgotten they are mortal.
Though the Name of the Lord
Is the most precious thing in the scriptures,
To that they attend not,
And they wander wildly like demons.
Saith Nānak: That man who hath discarded truth
And attached himself to falsehood hath gambled his life away.

xi

Those who, pure within, are also pure without,
Who are fair without and fair within, act virtuously,
Through the grace of the True Guru,
They have not heard even the name of falsehood;
All their hopes are set upon the Truth;
Blessed are such traders in virtue,
Who have earned the jewel of life.
Saith Nānak: Those who are pure within
Abide ever with the True Guru.

8

Soiled by its former births the soul is as black as jet:
Like an oily rag that could not be clean, were it washed a hundred
    times!
But if through the Guru's Grace a man dies to self
And be born to new understanding,
Then the soul is free from its soiling, and is not born again.

9

It is not they who burn themselves alive
With their husband's dead bodies, who are *Satīs*,
Nānak, they rather are Satīs,
Whom the shock of separation from their husbands kill;

They also are known as Satīs,
Who abide in modesty and contentment;
Who wait upon the Lord
And ever rising in the morning remember Him.

10

They are not truly husband and wife,
Whose bodies merely come together;
Only they are truly wedded
When two bodies have one soul.

13

Let no man be proud because of his caste.
For the man who graspeth God in his heart
He, no other, is the true Brahmin:
So, O fool, about thy caste be not vainglorious!
From vainglory emerge too many of the mind's evils!
Though they say there are four castes
One God created all men:
All men were moulded out of the same clay,
The Great Potter hath merely varied the shapes of them.
All men are mixed of the same five elements,
No one can make any element less in one, more in another.
Man is born in chains:
Without meeting the True Guru,
He cannot attain liberation.

Sikh Texts for a Wedding

1560s

Certain hymns in the Guru Granth *came to be seen as especially appropriate for particular occasions. Weddings in the Sikh community were (and are) celebrated by the bride and groom walking four times around the* Guru Granth, *a ceremony known as* lavan. *Each round was accompanied by specific verses, originally written by the fourth guru, Guru Ram Das, for his own wedding. In these verses, the soul of the believer is described as a bride seeking union with God, her "True Lord" and "Husband"; thus the word "she" applies to both the bride and the groom. Such marital imagery to describe the union of the believer and God is found in many of the world's religions, especially among mystics. What spiritual values are expressed in these wedding verses? How do marriage and family life appear to be valued?*

5.7.6.6 The Lavan

The first time round is the time for toil, for work in the world as the Lord may decree; || The Word of the Guru the text which we follow, confirming our faith and destroying our sin. || Be firm in believing and ponder God's Name, as prescribed by the scriptures of old. || Give to the Guru devout adoration, renouncing all evil and wrong. || Blessed is she who adores the Lord's Name, for its praises bring radiant bliss. || Nanak declares that the first of our rounds marks the start of our marriage with God.

The second time round is the time for our meeting, the meeting which comes with our only True Lord. || Fear is dispelled and our spirits are cleansed from the filth of our self-centred pride. || The fear we retain is our fear of the Lord as we sing to his praise and perceive him in all; || The Master is present in all his creation, his being pervading whatever we see. || Within and without he is ever our comrade;

Textual Sources for the Study of Sikhism, edited and translated by W. H. McLeod (Manchester: Manchester University Press, 1984), 118–19.

come join with his faithful and sing to his praise. || The mystical music resounds in our hearts as we follow the second round.

The third time round is the time for detachment, for freeing our minds from all worldly desire. || Blessed is she who unites with the faithful, for thus she is brought to her Lord. || She who finds God will sing hymns to his glory, the words which she utters inspired by her Lord. || Blessed is she who is found with the faithful, who utters the words of ineffable truth. || God's Name shall resound in the depths of her spirit, the Name we repeat if our fate so decrees. || The third round progresses, God rises within us, and cleanses our minds from all pride and desire.

Our spirits find peace as the fourth round commences, for God comes to dwell in our hearts and our minds. || By the grace of the Guru we know he is present, his sweetness pervading our bodies and souls. || This sweetness flows forth from the love which God nurtures for all who are rapt in his infinite bliss. || Desires they have treasured find precious reward at the sound of his glorious Name. || The bride who is chosen to marry her Lord knows that wonderful Name as it surges within. || Nanak declares that the fourth of our rounds brings our ultimate union with God.

That joy, my friend, so long desired is a joy I now possess; || For the Lord whom I sought to be my own has come and my heart is blest. || Wondrous the joy my Husband brings, ever-renewed his grace; || Blessed am I that the Guru has shown me God's presence amidst the devout. || In the midst of the faithful my hopes are fulfilled, my spirit at one with my Lord. || My prayers are all answered, joy I have found; joy by the Guru's grace.

I am joyously wed, O Father, having found my Lord by the Guru's grace. || Gone is the darkness of ignorant doubt, for the Guru has shown me his light. || The darkness flees as his light shines forth, the light which reveals my Lord. || The sickness of selfish conceit is cured, all pride consumed by his grace. || I have found my Lord, my immortal King, he who is free from the bondage of death. || I am joyously wed, O Father, having found my Lord by the Guru's grace.

5

East Asia: Competing and Combining Traditions in China and Japan

BACKGROUND

During the early modern era, several types of transformations in philosophical and religious systems occurred in China and Japan. In the Chinese Empire, the thought of the twelfth-century Confucian scholar Zhu Xi[1] was affirmed as the basis of an examination system for government officials, but was also criticized by dissenting scholars such as Wang Yangming and Li Zhi, who incorporated ideas from Buddhism and Daoism in their own thought. In Japan, Buddhism and Confucianism continued to blend with the indigenous religious tradition known as Shinto, though many learned officials increasingly favored Confucianism. In both countries, Catholic missionaries spread Christian teachings, but they were more successful in gaining converts in Japan.

China, the oldest empire in the world at this time, was ruled by the Ming dynasty, established in 1368 after the defeat of the Mongols, who had ruled China for a century. The founder of the Ming dynasty, usually known as the Hongwu emperor (ruled 1368–1398), reaffirmed Confucian philosophy, a system of beliefs that had been central in China since the Han dynasty (221 BCE–220 CE). Because it does not teach the worship of a god or gods, or have an organized structure, Confucianism is not exactly a religion, and is more accurately called a philosophy or way of life; it guides behavior and understandings about the world in the way that religions do elsewhere, however. Some Confucian scholars emphasized cosmic patterns beyond the human and natural worlds, patterns that they called the Principle or the Heavens or the Supreme Ultimate and hoped to experience through study and meditation; this form of Confucianism does seem

[1] choo shee.

to border on religious belief. The Ming dynasty collapsed in 1644, but Confucian ideas remained the most powerful force in China for many centuries afterwards.

Confucian ideas were also affirmed in Japan, a much smaller country than China with a less stable political system. Confucianism first entered Japan in the sixth century as part of a wave of Chinese influence and from that point on influenced many Japanese institutions. From the twelfth century, Japan was ruled by a military governor (*shogun*) through provincial lords. The lords relied on mounted warriors (*samurai*) to enforce and enhance their authority. Samurai were expected to live by a code of conduct later known as *bushido*[2] (the way of the warrior) that stressed honor, military values, and loyalty to their lord. In the sixteenth century samurai had plenty of opportunities to exhibit *bushido*, as there was constant warfare among lords. Toward the end of the century a series of military leaders gradually unified Japan, establishing what became known as the Tokugawa shogunate, which ruled the country until 1867. Tokugawa rulers were interested in Confucian thought and supported scholars who taught Confucian views.

Why were the ideas of Confucius (551–479 BCE) so attractive to Chinese and Japanese rulers? Confucius had lived during a turbulent period in Chinese history and decided that the best way to keep a society peaceful and prosperous was to make sure all positions of power were held by wise and honest men. These men should be sincere, ethical, and devoted to public service. They should show filial piety, which meant honoring their parents and ancestors. Rulers should have these qualities, and they should surround themselves with advisers who were also wise and moral. Under the leadership of such advisers, society would be a well-ordered hierarchy in which everyone was arranged in ranks and knew their place. The educated would rule the common people, parents would rule their children, and men would rule women. This emphasis on hierarchy and respect for authority had obvious appeal to those who held power and in Japan fit with the principle of loyalty to one's superior in *bushido*.

Confucianism was only one of many philosophical/religious systems in China and Japan. Many people followed traditional religions with multiple gods and spirits. In Japan, this indigenous religion came to be called *Shinto*, and the Japanese emperor was regarded as the descendant of one of these gods, the Sun Goddess Amaterasu.

[2]boo-SHEE-doh.

Daoism, which like Confucianism had ancient origins, taught that one should simply accept the world as it is and adhere to the "path" (*dao*) of nature. Daoism[3] began in China and spread into Japan about the same time Confucianism did; in both places Daoists often blended in traditional popular beliefs and practices of spirit worship. Buddhism first spread into China in the first century and into Japan (by way of Korea) in the sixth century, bringing with it more elaborate theories about the working of the cosmos than Confucianism or Daoism offered. Buddhist thought also tended to dismiss earthly affairs as distractions and supported the establishment of monasteries where men and women lived cut off from the world to some degree. This stood in sharp contrast to the Confucian emphasis on doing one's duty to family, community, and the larger world.

Buddhism was attractive to many people, including some rulers, and during the Song dynasty (960–1279) in China several Confucian scholars developed more complex metaphysical theories in response to Buddhism. These scholars are sometimes called *neo-Confucian*, but this is a Western term; Song Confucian scholars did not think they were doing anything new but simply reviving a way that was closer to the original. In this they sound much like Luther, who also saw his reforms as a return to original ideals. The most important of these Song Confucians was Zhu Xi (1130–1200), who held that everything in the universe results from the interaction of *qi*[4] (vital force) and *li* (rational principle). This interaction creates the *wu xing*,[5] five forces through which *qi* brings about change in the world, and the complementary opposing forces yin and yang. Together yin and yang form the *Taiji*,[6] or Supreme Ultimate, a dynamic principle linked to *li* that operates within the individual (akin to the spirit or mind) and in all things in the universe. Similar ideas can be found in Daoism and Buddhism, but Zhu Xi asserted that they can also be found in writings attributed to Confucius. He gathered these writings into groups that came to be considered the Confucian classics, and wrote long commentaries on them. Zhu Xi taught that attaining wisdom came best through the "investigation of things," that is, the study of historical events for meaningful patterns of human behavior. Such study would provide moral guidance and perhaps allow one to become a sage, an individual with perfect moral behavior. Like Confucius himself, Zhu Xi

[3] DOW-izm.
[4] chee.
[5] woo SHING.
[6] ty-CHEE.

was not recognized during his lifetime, but in later centuries his synthesis of Confucian learning and his commentaries, termed the *School of Principle*, became the officially accepted interpretation of Confucius and the basis for the state educational system.

The Ming dynasty emperors enhanced the authority of Confucian scholars and expanded the system of imperial civil-service examinations based on Confucian classics through which men could rise in the ranks of officials. The development of woodblock-printed books dramatically lowered the cost of books and broadened access to texts at all educational levels. From the fourteenth century through the early twentieth, boys (or their families) hoping to gain the government salary, official position, and special title that success in the national examinations could bring studied in academies and universities all over China. They studied the works of Zhu Xi and other classics to provide content for their examination essays and also practiced calligraphy, poetry, and composition so that the form of their essay would catch the eye of examiners and allow it to rise above those of the tens of thousands of other students competing for the same opportunities. Candidates thus imbibed a state-sanctioned form of Confucianism and were generally the type of loyal, conservative bureaucrats that the emperors hoped they would be.

In the sixteenth century, however, critics began to charge that this educational system promoted a superficial and empty following of rules, a mere pretense of ethics and moral behavior rather than true virtue. Their criticisms sound very similar to those of Erasmus about European Christianity and the Sikh gurus about religious practice in South Asia. Some of these dissenting Confucian scholars turned away from the connection with the outside world and advocated a more inner directed philosophy. Wang Yangming had a tumultuous career as an official and military general, undergoing exile at one point. He began to doubt whether the "investigation of things" would ever lead to true sagehood, for how could one ever know enough? He decided that the best way to understand morality was not studying events, nor even studying the classics, but by practicing inward contemplation. Meditative techniques could help one come to know Heaven (*Xian*), which Wang viewed as a divine consciousness or divine will, not a place. Every person knows the difference between right and wrong, Wang argued, and through developing their innate intuitive knowledge—what he called knowledge of the mind and heart—ordinary people could become as wise as scholars. Wang's ideas came to be known as the School of the Mind (mind in Chinese thought is associated with the heart, not the head, so mind and heart are one) and is distinguished from the School of Principle associated with Zhu Xi. (See Documents 34 and 35.)

Wang's individualistic emphasis upset many scholar-bureaucrats but inspired others, such as Li Zhi, a brilliant iconoclastic thinker who challenged Confucian beliefs and values. Though he was a bright young man, Li never took the highest level of examination and held only lower-level official positions throughout his career. Such positions gave him plenty of time to study and think. Later in life he resigned his position and entered a Buddhist monastery, leaving his wife and children. He never took up normal monastic duties but wrote essays, letters, poems, and other works asserting that Confucianism, Buddhism, and Daoism were essentially the same. He argued that the emotions, as well as meditation or study, could teach moral truths, an idea that most Confucian officials regarded as dangerous. (See Documents 36 and 37.) Li knew his works repudiated conventional morality and teachings—he titled one of them *A Book to Burn* and another *A Book to Be Hidden Away*—but he persisted, even after a mob burned down the house where his family was living. Finally the emperor ordered him arrested and his books burned; Li committed suicide while in jail.

Li's ideas, and those of Wang Yangming and other dissenters from the state-approved version of Confucianism, continued to spread through written texts, however, and were sometimes taught at private academies. Artists were inspired by this intellectual movement to challenge traditional views of art upheld by the state-sanctioned academies. Some artists refused to follow accepted methods, styles, and forms, but created intense works of personal interpretation incorporating Daoist and Buddhist ideas, which more traditional painters judged "eccentric" or even "degenerate." (See Document 38.)

The ideas of Wang Yangming spread to Japan as well, as part of a new wave of Confucianism during the early modern period. The more powerful voices here, however, were those promoting orthodox Confucian thought and the teachings of Zhu Xi. One such voice was that of scholar and official Hayashi Razan (1583–1657). Razan became an official adviser to the Tokugawa shoguns, who gave him money and land to build a school. He and other writers emphasized that Confucianism fit well with *bushido*, which also centered on loyalty toward one's superiors, and with Shinto, the traditional Japanese religion. (See Document 39.) Some Japanese Confucians argued, in fact, that the Japanese were better Confucians than were the Chinese, as they honored their lords and their parents more completely. The military leaders who were gradually unifying Japan saw Buddhist institutions, especially the wealthy and powerful monasteries, as rivals; Oda Nobunaga (1534–1582), the first of these leaders, burned the largest Buddhist monastery in Japan to the ground and slaughtered many of its 20,000 inhabitants.

At the same time that Confucian thinkers in China and Japan were debating the role of innate thoughts versus learned knowledge, and discussing (or acting on) the similarities and differences among Confucianism, Daoism, Buddhism, and Shinto, Catholic missionaries came to East Asia, first to Portuguese Macao, and then to China and Japan. The Italian Jesuit Matteo Ricci (1552–1610) impressed the Chinese imperial court with his learning, but Catholic missionaries had little lasting impact in China.

Political disunity in Japan gave Christian missionaries in 1549 more opportunities than they found in China. Jesuits, beginning with Francis Xavier (1506–1552), presented Christianity as a unified system of faith and practice, not revealing that it was in the midst of enormous upheaval, reformation, and splintering in Europe; this unity made it particularly appealing at a time of warfare and disruption. They built churches, set up confraternities, trained indigenous assistants, and began to train an indigenous clergy. Their converts included women as well as men, who played active roles as catechists, baptizers, and teachers. (See Document 40.) Some members of the nobility declared they were Christians, often ordering their subjects to receive baptism as well. For some nobles, the primary attraction to Christianity was the access missionaries provided to European trade goods and military technology, but for others the appeal included the Christian ethical code and notion of absolute obedience to an ultimate god. Common people, especially in the southern Japanese island of Kyushu, converted as well, drawn by the Christian idea of a transcendent salvation and moral teachings. By 1580 there were more than 100,000 Christians in Japan and by 1610 perhaps as many as 300,000, a higher percentage of the Japanese population at that time than during any later period.

Oda Nobunaga initially tolerated Christianity, in part because of his opposition to traditional Buddhism. Toyotomi Hideyoshi (1536–1598), Nobunaga's successor as unifier of Japan, became convinced, however, that Christians were intent on military conquest and overthrowing the government. (See Document 41.) In this he was influenced by Protestant Dutch and English traders who opposed the Jesuits on religious grounds and were trying to lessen Portuguese trading power. In 1587, Hideyoshi passed an order expelling all Catholic priests, though it was not rigorously enforced and conversions continued. A second order in 1614, composed by Hayashi Razan and other officials at the shogun's court, ordered all Christians, Japanese and foreign, to leave or convert. Some did leave, often going to the Spanish-held Philippines, and some did convert. Many others could not leave and would not convert, maintaining their faith despite arrests, gruesome torture, and execution. The Shimabara Rebellion of 1637–1638, in which peasants protested their conditions, was led by Japanese Christians in Kyushu; this resulted in a final exclusion order of 1639 banning any further visits by Portuguese ships or interaction with Catholic lands. In 1641 all contact with Europeans was limited to a small island in the Nagasaki harbor run by the Dutch East India Company. Many historians think that the perceived threat of Christianity was a central factor in Japan's decision to implement a "closed door" policy, which lasted until the 1860s. Japan had absorbed and blended Confucianism, Daoism, and Buddhism, but Christianity, which demanded sole allegiance, could not become part of this mixture.

Japanese rulers assumed they had obliterated Christianity, but despite an extensive system of surveillance with monetary rewards offered for the exposure of Christians, Christianity survived as an underground religion in remote farming and fishing villages of northern Kyushu and some smaller islands. These "hidden Christians" had no clergy, but lay leaders secretly taught, kept records, and baptized; they maintained their community by marrying within the group and gradually developed a distinctive version of Christianity, often using Buddhist images that presented themes similar to those in Christianity to avoid detection. When Japan was reopened in the 1860s, these Japanese Christians contacted Catholic priests, who were astounded to learn of their existence.

The stories of Confucianism and Christianity in Tokugawa Japan are compelling examples of the various types of religious transformations found in many places in the early modern world. These transformations led to creative synthesis, deeply felt conversion, and harsh opposition—developments that you have no doubt found elsewhere as you have read the documents in this book.

DOCUMENTS

Writings by learned scholars supporting and criticizing Confucianism circulated in many forms in Ming China, as handwritten letters, manuscripts that were copied, and books printed with woodblocks. Printing first became commercially important in the twelfth century in China, when enterprising printers produced expensive encyclopedias and editions of Confucian classics along with much cheaper books of commentary, poetry, and how-to manuals. Printing helped the writings of Zhu Xi to become widely influential in both China and Japan, where Confucian officials translated them into very formal Japanese and then into more informal styles. In the sixteenth century in China, as every aspiring examination candidate sought to make his essay distinct from others, printed commentaries by many authors also provided quotes and models that suggested new understandings of traditional works.

This diversity fit well with Wang Yangming's notion that each person had an innate understanding of what was right. Some historians see the increased circulation of ideas that printing allowed as an important background factor in the individualistic challenge to authority of thinkers such as Wang Yangming and Li Zhi, just as printing in Europe allowed wider circulation of criticism of the Catholic Church. Wang Yangming's writings were taken to Japan, where some scholars accepted his ideas, attracted by the emphasis on intuitive moral reasoning. They were vigorously attacked as too individualistic by the scholars who were most influential at court, however, who eventually succeeded in having all schools of Confucianism except that of Zhu Xi banned.

Christianity in early modern Japan also produced a range of sources. As in Mesoamerica, missionaries worked with indigenous converts to translate catechisms, books of the Bible, and other devotional literature, and trained artists to make pictures and objects that would spread the Christian message visually. There are also a number of written works by Japanese people who listened and responded to the missionaries, so that it is easier to learn about their ideas directly than it is for Mesoamerica, where nearly all written materials, including those in Nahuatl, were produced by missionaries and their allies.

As you examine these sources, you can identify and compare the way the main themes emerge in them. Confucianism does not teach the worship of a specific god or gods. How does this shape the ideas of Wang Yangming, Li Zhi, and Hayashi Razan? (See Documents 34–37 and 39.) Hayashi Razan supports the state-sanctioned Confucianism of Zhu Xi, while Wang Yangming, Li Zhi, and the artist Kuncan (Document 38) present a more individualistic understanding. On what key points do differences between these two variants emerge? What do all the Confucian writings agree on? Hayashi Razan and Hideyoshi (Document 41) both discuss the blending of religious traditions in Japan. On what points do they agree, and on what do they differ? Li Zhi (Document 37) and Hosokawa Tama Gracia (Document 40) both describe spiritual activities by women; what similarities and differences do you see in their views of the ideal female believer? Do they appear to view ideal male religious behavior as different from this? (For questions that relate these sources to those in other chapters in the book, see p. 163.)

34

WANG YANGMING

Questions on the Great Learning

1527

The Great Learning *was one of the books that Zhu Xi designated in the twelfth century as a central Confucian text; he and later Confucian scholars, including Wang Yangming, wrote commentaries on it. The* Great Learning *describes the way that ancient sage-kings attained the highest good. For Zhu Xi, this was a gradual process achieved through long methodical study and contemplation, possible only for elites. Wang Yangming had a different opinion. Where does he locate the highest good, and as a result of this, how does he view human nature? How are people to achieve this highest good?*

People fail to realize that the highest good is in their minds and seek it outside. As they believe that everything or every event has its own definite principle, they search for the utmost good in individual things. Consequently, the mind becomes fragmented, isolated, broken into pieces. Mixed and confused, it has no definite direction. Once it is realized that the utmost good is in the mind and does not depend on any search outside, then the mind will have definite direction and

Sources of Chinese Tradition, 2nd ed., compiled by Wm. Theodore de Bary and Irene Bloom (New York: Columbia University Press, 1999), 845–47.

there will be no danger of its becoming fragmented, isolated, broken into pieces, mixed, or confused.

Now the original substance of the mind is human nature. Human nature being universally good, the original substance of the mind is correct. How is it that any effort is required to rectify the mind? The reason is that, while the original substance of the mind is originally correct, incorrectness enters when one's thoughts and intentions are in operation. Therefore one who wishes to rectify one's mind must rectify it in connection with the operation of one's thoughts and intention. If, whenever a good thought arises, one really loves it as one loves beautiful colors, and whenever an evil thought arises, one really hates it as one hates bad odors, then one's intention will always be sincere and one's mind can be rectified. . . .

The extension of knowledge is not what later scholars understand as enriching and widening knowledge. It is simply extending one's innate knowing to the utmost. This innate knowing is what Mencius[1] meant when he said, "The sense of right and wrong is common to all human beings." The sense of right and wrong requires no deliberation to know, nor does it depend on learning to function. This is why it is called innate knowing. It is my nature endowed by Heaven, the original substance of my mind, naturally intelligent, shining, clear, and understanding. . . .

As the utmost good emanates and reveals itself, we will consider right as right and wrong as wrong. Things of greater or less importance and situations of grave or light character will be responded to as they act upon us. In all our changes and movements, we will stick to no particular point but possess in ourselves the Mean that is perfectly natural. This is the ultimate of the normal nature of man and the principle of things. There can be no consideration of adding to or subtracting anything from it—such a suggestion reveals selfish ideas and shallow cunning and cannot be said to be the utmost good. Naturally, how can anyone who does not watch over himself carefully when alone, and who lacks refined discrimination and unity, attain to such a state of perfection? Later generations fail to realize that the utmost good is inherent in their own minds, but exercise their selfish ideas and cunning and grope for it outside their minds, believing that every event and every object has its own peculiar and definite principle.

---

[1]*Mencius* (372–289 BCE): Influential spokesman for Confucian ideas.

35

WANG YANGMING

The Community Compact for Southern Ganzhou

1520s

Wang Yangming did not develop his ideas in scholarly seclusion, but while serving as an official and general responsible for subduing rebels and outlaws in Jianxi province in southern China. His career was thus a model of one of his key ideas, that knowing and acting should be unified. Zhu Xi, by contrast, had argued that knowledge should come first, then action. Wang decided not to punish former rebels but attempt to turn them into model citizens. He called for "community compacts," agreements between community members, including former outlaws, in which all pledged to act in a moral fashion and police their own behavior. These compacts, as in this example from the city of Ganzhou in Jianxi province, established procedures for those who broke the rules, but Wang urged greater attention be paid to good deeds than to mistakes. What kind of behavior does Wang prescribe for those who are to live morally? How does the structure of leadership in the compact reflect Confucian ideals?

In the past, new citizens have often deserted their own clans, rebelled against their own community, and gone in all directions to do violence. Was this merely because their nature was different and they were criminals? It was also because, on our part, the government did not govern them properly or teach them in the right way, and on your part, all of you, both old and young, did not reach and regulate your families early enough or exert good influence on your fellow villagers regularly enough. You did not put inducement and encouragement into practice and had no sufficient arrangements for cooperation and coordination. . . .

Alas! Nothing can be done to change what has already gone by, but something can still be done in the future. Therefore a community compact is now specially prepared to unite and harmonize all of you. From now on, all of you who enter into this compact should be filial to

Sources of Chinese Tradition, 2nd ed., compiled by Wm. Theodore de Bary and Irene Bloom (New York: Columbia University Press, 1999), 854–55.

your parents and respectful to your elders, teach your children, live in harmony with your fellow villagers, help one another when there is death in the family and assist one another in times of difficulty, encourage one another to do good and warn one another not to do evil, stop litigations and rivalry, cultivate faithfulness and promote harmony, and be sure to be good citizens so that together you may establish the custom of humanity and kindness. Alas! Although a man is most stupid, when it comes to criticizing others his mind is quite clear, and although a person is quite intelligent, when it comes to criticizing himself his mind is beclouded. All of you, both old and young, should not remember the former evil deeds of the new citizens and ignore their good deeds. As long as they have a single thought to do good, they are already good people. Do not be proud that you are good citizens and neglect to cultivate your personal life. As long as you have a single thought to do evil, you are already evil people. Whether people are good or evil depends on a single instant of thought. You should think over my words carefully. Don't forget.

Item: Elect from the compact membership an elderly and virtuous person respected by all to be the compact chief and two persons to be assistant chiefs, four persons who are impartial, just, and firm in judgment to be compact directors, four persons who are understanding and discriminating to be compact recorders, four persons who are energetic and scrupulous to be compact executives, and two persons who are well versed in ceremonies to be compact masters of ceremonies. Have three record books. One of these is to record the names of compact members and their daily movements and activities, and is to be in the charge of the compact executives. Of the remaining record books, one is for the purpose of displaying good deeds and the other for the purpose of reporting evil deeds, both to be in the charge of the compact chief. . . .

Item: To display good deeds, the language used must be clear and decisive, but in reporting mistakes, the language must be indirect and gentle.

36

LI ZHI

A Book to Burn (Fenshu)
1590

Li Zhi[1] spent most of his life as a minor official but eventually quit his position and went to live in a Buddhist monastery. There he wrote many works that repudiated traditional Confucian teachings and in 1590 published a collection of these that he titled A Book to Burn. *According to Li, what did Confucius teach about where true humanity comes from? How does Li view efforts by scholars and the state to impose moral principles on people? Given what he says here, why might he have given the book the title that he did?*

Each human being Heaven gives birth to . . . has his own individual function and he does not need to learn this from Confucius. If he did need to learn this from Confucius, how then, in all the ages before Confucius, could anyone have achieved their full humanity? . . .

Confucius never taught people to study Confucius. If he had taught them to study Confucius, why is it that when Yan Yuan asked about humaneness, Confucius answered that one achieves humaneness in and through one's self, not through others? Why is it that Confucius said, "In ancient times learning was for one's self [not for the sake of others]," and said, "The noble person seeks it in himself"? Because it was from the self, his followers did not need to ask Confucius about humaneness. Because it was for one's self, his teaching of others was based on his own self-study. . . .

To wear clothing and eat food—these are the principles of human relations. Without them there are no human relations. . . . The scholar should learn only what is real and unreal in respect to these relations and not impose other principles of human relations on top of them. . . .

[1] lee SHEE.

Sources of Chinese Tradition, 2nd ed., compiled by Wm. Theodore de Bary and Irene Bloom (New York: Columbia University Press, 1999), 867–68, 870, 873.

People have always found their own natural place [when left alone]. If they do not it is only because they are harassed by those who are greedy and aggressive and harmed by humanitarians.[2] The humanitarians worry about everyone finding his place in the world, and so they have virtue and rites to correct people's minds, and the state with its punishments to fetter their limbs. Then people begin to lose their place in a big way! . . .

Once people's minds have been given over to received opinions and moral principles, what they have to say is all about these things, and not what would naturally come from their childlike minds. No matter how clever the words, what have they to do with oneself? What else can there be but phony men speaking phony words, doing phony things, writing phony writings? Once the men become phonies, everything becomes phony. Thereafter, if one speaks phony talk to the phonies, the phonies are pleased; if one does phony things as the phonies do, the phonies are pleased; and if one discourses with the phonies through phony writings, the phonies are pleased. Everything is phony, and everyone is pleased.

[2] *humanitarians*: Confucian scholar-bureaucrats.

37

LI ZHI

Two Letters

1590s

Li Zhi attracted students and followers who proposed to follow his example and retreat from the world by becoming Buddhist monks. The following letters contain his advice to two such men. In the first letter, what does Li Zhi advise the young man to do? How do Confucian ideals of filial piety shape his advice? The second quotes a letter to Ruowu, one of his students contemplating a move to a more isolated monastery, from his mother. (We have no way of knowing if the mother's letter is real or if

Patricia Ebrey, *Chinese Civilization: A Sourcebook* (New York: Free Press, 1993), 259–61.

Li Zhi simply invents it as a way to get his point across.) Why does Ruowu's mother object to this move? What religious/philosophical concepts does she use in her argument? In his comments on this letter, Li Zhi notes that this woman is a "real Buddha." Why does he call her this? Based on these two letters, how would Li Zhi define ideal masculine behavior? Based on his discussion of Ruowu's mother, how might he define ideal feminine behavior?

To Zeng Jiquan[1]

I hear that you intend to shave your hair and become a monk. You really should not do so.

You have a wife and concubines, as well as a house and land. What is more, you do not yet have a son. Now, without a son, to whom are you going to entrust your family and possessions? To desert them without a reason is not only unkind but irresponsible. If you have really transcended life and death and seen through human existence, then it is preferable to cultivate yourself at home.

I should like to ask you some hypothetical questions: Can you really hold a monk's bowl to beg for food from door to door? Or can you really fast for several days without begging for a meal from people? If you can do neither, but still have to rely on farming for a livelihood, then isn't it more practical to cultivate yourself at home?

In the beginning, when I had just started studying the [Buddhist] Way, not only did I have a wife and family, I also was an official who had to travel tens of thousands of *li*.[2] But I felt that my learning increased day by day. Later on, I stayed in Chu to be close to my good friends and teachers, but my wife would not stay with me; I had to let my son-in-law and my daughter accompany her home. There she had her daughter, nephew, and others waiting on her constantly. I handed over to her whatever savings I had from my offices. As I alone was away from home, I did not need to worry about her and was able to stay down here and enjoy the company of my friends. The reason why I shaved my hair was that various people at home always expected me to return and often actually traveled a thousand *li* to pressure me to return and to bother me with trivial, worldly affairs. So I shaved my hair to show them that I had no intention of returning. Also, the

---

[1]tsung chee-KWAN.
[2]*li*: A measure of distance, about three miles.

ignorant people down here eyed me as a heretic, so I let myself behave as such to satisfy them. And yet was my sudden decision to shave my hair based primarily on these reasons? In addition, I knew I was getting old and would not stay in this world of men for long; that was the true reason. Now you, sir, are in your prime years, the fittest time to beget children, to live, to aspire for greatness. Furthermore, you do not own too much land and your estate is not very large. This is the ideal condition in which to live—unlike those rich men who are tied down with so many financial worries that they do not have even one minute of leisure.

Now, tell me, why do you have to discard your hair in order to learn the Way? I, for one, did not get rid of mine and leave home when I started studying it. Do mark my words and bear them in mind.

On Reading the Letter to Ruowu[3] from His Mother

Ruowu's mother wrote to him, "I am getting older year after year. I have been a widow since you were eight and have brought you up. You left me to become a monk and that was all right. But now you want to leave in another sense to go to Jingang. Even your teacher waited until his parents passed away before becoming a monk. If you want to go away, you can wait until I have died. It will not be too late then.

"You say that even when you live close to me, you have never been able to help me in any way. Yet, when I am ill or indisposed, it is convenient to have you around. That way I do not worry about you. You also are carefree, not having to worry about me. Thus we both live with peace of mind, and where there is peace of mind there is tranquillity. Why are you set on leaving home to seek for quiet? Besides, Qin Suge, who has always been generous to you, has bought you the temple. You always think in terms of the Way; I, however, think in terms of the ways of the world. I believe that what harmonizes with the ways of the world also conforms to the Way.

"Now, even if you forget about my old age, you have an obligation to care for your two small children. Even after your teacher became a monk, he took care of his sons during the famine years. This was because he could not put them out of his mind. For should he have failed to take care of them, they would have become roving good-for-nothings and the butt of insults and ridicule.

[3]roo-OH-woo.

"Now you want to cultivate sereneness of the mind, but are you going to be concerned about your children? I do not believe you can be unconcerned about them. The fact is that you are concerned, but out of fear of being ridiculed by others, you hide your feelings. Let me ask you this: which is more honest, which is better, 'concerned but refusing to be involved,' or 'concerned and involved'? The way I see it, if you take care of your children, although it may seem that you are concerned, yet because you can thus achieve peace of mind, you are actually not concerned. On the other hand, if you do not take care of them, you are seemingly unconcerned, yet because your mind feels secret pangs, you are in fact concerned. You ought to examine your own mind. If you can achieve a peaceful mind, then that is the eternal dwelling place, that is the Jingang you are looking for.

"Why do you only listen to others? To listen to others and not to examine your own mind is to be manipulated by circumstances. Once you submit to that, there will be no peace of mind for you. . . . I fear for you: You now find Longtan not quiet enough and wish to go to live in Jingang. Should you someday find Jingang not quiet enough, where else are you going to go? You always talk only of the 'Way'; I wish now to talk to you about 'mind.' If you do not believe me, ask your teacher. If what matters is the surroundings, then you should indeed go and dwell in Jingang. If what matters is the mind, however, then you have no need to go away. If your mind is not serene, then even if you should travel to the other side of the sea, you would still not find quiet, let alone in Jingang."

On reading the letter, I sighed. I congratulate you on having a mother who is a real Buddha. From morning till night you have with you a teacher of the mind. She speaks with the voice of the ocean tide and teaches the ultimate truth which can never be contradicted. In comparison, the rhetoric of our peers is neither to the point nor effective. We are like those who talk about food, acting as though we could feed people with our mere words. All we achieve is making people laugh at each other, yet we do not even feel ashamed of ourselves. In retrospect, I realize that the several pages I wrote to you were mere exaggerations which would impress the foolish but had no bearing whatsoever on the truth. I now beg you to destroy my letters so that your godly mother may not read them, lest she say that I have spent all my life expounding harmful ideas. I also wish you would circulate your mother's letter and make students of Buddhism read it from time to time, so that they will learn to study true Buddhism. As long as one studies true Buddhism, one is a real Buddha.

38

KUNCAN (K'UN-TS'AN)

Wooded Mountains at Dusk
1666

Kuncan (1612–1673) was an educated poet-painter who retreated from urban society to enter a Buddhist monastery but frequently traveled to paint landscapes directly from nature. His paintings often portray tiny figures in a dramatic natural setting and frequently include poetic inscriptions. In this painting, a traveler walks on stones across a river at the bottom, and the painter himself is almost invisible under a stone bridge near the top. The poem in the upper right reads:

> I want to go further,
> But my legs are bruised and scratched.
> The bony rocks appear chiseled,
> The pines look as if they had been dyed.
> Sitting down, I feel like a small bird,
> As I look out at the crowd of peaks gathered before me.
> Having ascended the heights to the brink of the abyss,
> I hold fast and ponder the need to sincerely face criticism.
> Wherever a road ends, I will set myself down,
> Wherever a source opens, I will build a temple.
> All this suffices to nourish my eyes,
> And rest my feet.

How does this painting reflect Wang Yangming's notion of the unity of the human and natural world and Li Zhi's idea of the power of the senses? In what ways does the artist blend concepts from different traditions?

150

39

HAYASHI RAZAN

Ruling and Living in Conformity with the Order of Heaven and Earth

ca. 1620

Hayashi Razan[1] was an official at the Tokugawa court and established a hereditary line of Confucian advisers to the shoguns. He and his successors wrote history as well as philosophical and political works, which, not surprisingly, played up the impact of their ideas. In this selection, he affirms traditional Confucian ideas, which were being challenged in Japan by other thinkers who accepted the more individualistic and Buddhist-influenced Confucianism of Wang Yangming and Li Zhi. What cosmic patterns provide a model for human social and political relationships? How does Confucianism fit, in Razan's opinion, with Shinto, the indigenous Japanese religion?

Natural Order and Social Order

The Principle (*ri*, or in Chinese *li*) which existed constantly before and after heaven and earth came into being is called the Supreme Ultimate. When this Supreme Ultimate was in motion, it created the *yang*, and when it was quiescent, it created the *yin*. The *yin* and *yang* were originally of the same substance but were divided into two complementary forces. They were further divided into the Five Elements which are wood, fire, earth, metal and water. When the Five Elements were further divided, they became all things under heaven. When these Five Elements were brought together to take shapes, people were also born.

All creatures existing between heaven and earth were shaped by the Five Elements. However, because of the difference in the Ether, there emerged plants, animals and men. . . .

---

[1] ha-YAH-shee RAH-zahn.

David Lu, *Japan: A Documentary History* (Armonk, N.Y.: M. E. Sharpe, 1997), 245–47.

A concrete object comes into being because of the work of heaven and earth. All creatures, plants, animals and inanimate objects owe their existence to the will of heaven and earth. Thus not a single object lacks within it the principles of heaven. . . .

Therefore the Five Constant Virtues of human-heartedness, righteousness, propriety, wisdom, and good faith are given by heaven and exist on account of the principles of heaven. . . .

The five relationships governing the ruler and the subject, father and son, husband and wife, older brother and younger brother, and friend and friend have been in existence from olden days to the present time. There has been no change in these basic relations, and they are thus called the supreme way. In judging the worth of a person, one needs only to use these five relationships as the criteria, and teachings which try to implement the ideals of these five relationships are those of the sage and of the wise men. . . .

Heaven is above and earth is below. This is the order of heaven and earth. If we can understand the meaning of the order existing between heaven and earth, we can also perceive that in everything there is an order separating those who are above and those who are below. When we extend this understanding between heaven and earth, we cannot allow disorder in the relations between the ruler and the subject, and between those who are above and those who are below. The separation into four classes of samurai, farmers, artisans and merchants, like the five relationships, is part of the principles of heaven and is the Way which was taught by the Sage (Confucius). . . .

To know the way of heaven is to respect heaven and to secure humble submission from earth, for heaven is high above and earth is low below. There is a differentiation between the above and the below. Likewise among the people, rulers are to be respected and subjects are to submit humbly. Only when this differentiation between those who are above and those who are below is made clear, can there be law and propriety. In this way, people's minds can be satisfied. . . . The more the rulers are respected, and the more the subjects submit humbly, and the more the differentiation is made clear-cut, the easier it is to govern a country. Among the rulers, there are the Emperor, the *shogun*, and the *daimyo*, and even among them there is also differentiation. . . .

On the Unity of Shinto and Confucianism

Our country is the country of gods. Shinto is the same as the Way of the King. However, the rise of Buddhism made the people abandon the Way of the King and Shinto. Someone may ask how Shinto and

Confucianism can be differentiated. I respond by saying that according to my observation the Principle (*ri*) is the same, but only its application differs. . . .

In comparing the books on the age of gods in the *Nihonshoki* (Chronicles of Japan) with Master Chou's (Chou Tun-yi, 1017–1073) *T'ai-chi T'ushuo* (Diagram of the Supreme Ultimate Explained), I have yet to find any discrepancy in substantive matters. The Way of the King transforms itself into Shinto and Shinto transforms itself into Way. What I mean by the term "Way" is the Way of Confucianism, and it is not the so-called alien doctrine. The alien doctrine is Buddhism.

40

HOSOKAWA TAMA GRACIA

Letter to the Jesuit Superior Gregorio de Cespedes
1590

Hosokawa Tama Gracia[1] *(1565?–1600) was the daughter of a powerful lord, married while she was a teenager to Hosokawa Tadaoki, another high-ranking noble in the period during which Japan was slowly being unified through constant warfare. She was highly learned in many of the religious traditions of Japan, particularly in Buddhism, and first heard about Christianity from another noble who had converted. Though her husband ordered her to remain in the house while he was away fighting, she surreptitiously visited the Jesuit mission and debated religious issues with several missionaries. Leaving the house again was too dangerous, but one of her ladies-in-waiting continued to visit the Jesuits, communicating Tama Gracia's questions and returning with Christian literature in Japanese. This lady-in-waiting was baptized by the Jesuits and took the name Maria. In 1587, right after the initial edict ordering the Jesuits to leave Japan, Maria baptized Tama Gracia. Tama Gracia, Maria, and several other court ladies learned to read and write Portuguese, and*

---

[1] hoh-soh-KAH-wah TAH-mah GRAH-tsee-uh.

C. R. Boxer, "Hosokawa Tadaoki and the Jesuits, 1587–1645," in *Portuguese Merchants and Missionaries in Feudal Japan, 1543–1640*, ed. C. R. Boxer (Ashgate: Variorum, 1986), IV:88–89.

Tama Gracia corresponded regularly with the Jesuits. The following is a letter that she wrote to Gregorio de Cespedes,[2] who was a Jesuit mission-ary in Japan from 1577 to his death in 1611. How does Tama Gracia describe her conversion? Why does she think that her husband is treating the women of her household harshly? What does she see as the proper role of a female Christian convert? Her own fate turned out to be similar to what she hoped for at the end of this letter, although not for the reasons she expected. While her husband was away on a military campaign, sol-diers from a rival faction in the civil wars surrounded the house. After sending her servants and court ladies away, Tama Gracia ordered her husband's samurai to kill her rather than allow her to be captured, the behavior expected of a Japanese noble woman according to the code of bushido. Tama Gracia also came to be revered as a Christian martyr, however, and the anniversary of her death was celebrated with elaborate memorial ceremonies for a number of years.

As for myself, Your Reverence well knows how I was made a Chris-tian, not at the persuasion of men, but only by the grace and mercy of the one all-powerful God, whom I have found. Even if the heavens should fall to earth and the trees and herbs cease to grow, I, by the confidence I have in Him, will never change. Very grievous is the mishap which befell us in this persecution of the Fathers, but the faith of good Christians is thereby proved. After the departure of the Fathers there has been no lack of trials for me, but in everything God has favoured and supported me. My second son (a babe of three years) was very ill, and when there was no longer any hope of his recovery, I, dreading greatly the loss of his soul, consulted with Maria what to do, and we found that the best remedy would be to entrust him to the God who has created him. Maria therefore secretly bap-tised him and christened him John, and from that very day he began to recover, and he is now completely cured. Yechundono,[3] after he had returned from the war, as he is exceedingly severe in his mode of life, took a nurse of one of my sons (who was likewise baptised) and for a very small fault cut off her ears and nose and threw her out of the house. Subsequently he cut the hair off two others and expelled them, since all three were Christians. I have been careful to furnish them

[2] de seh-SPEH-dess.
[3] *Yechundono*: Her husband.

with all necessary things, and send to encourage them to persevere in the faith. These few days past Yechundono went to the kingdom of Tango; before his departure he told me that on his return he intended to make a certain enquiry in this household, and we suspect that it must be about the Law of God and there being in the house some Christian converts. Maria and I are prepared for any persecution whencesoever it comes, whether from Yechundono or from Quambacudono,[4] and we would rejoice if on this score we could suffer something for the love of God. I am always very desirous of hearing news of the Fathers and hope that Our Lord will bring them back here to help me save my children. I beg of them, if they have the chance, not to lose any opportunity of writing to me, as also of commending me in their prayers and Mass. All the Christians whom I have with me are strong, and I work in exhorting them to martyrdom, if perchance we may be found worthy of so great a thing. From Vozàca, the seventh of the eleventh moon.

[4] *Quambacudono*: Hideyoshi, one of the unifiers of Japan.

41

TOYOTOMI HIDEYOSHI

Letter to the Viceroy of the Indies
1591

The expulsion of Jesuit missionaries in 1587 provoked reactions on the part of European Catholic officials. The viceroy of the Indies, a Portuguese official in charge of the colony at Goa, wrote to Toyotomi Hideyoshi[1] in protest. This is Hideyoshi's reply, which first describes his role in unifying Japan and his ambitions to conquer China, and then turns to religious issues. How does Hideyoshi view the relationship among Japan's three major religious traditions: Confucianism, Buddhism, and

[1] toh-yoh-TOE-mee hee-deh-YOH-shee.

Ryusaku Tsunoda, Wm. Theodore de Bary, and Donald Keene, eds., *Sources of Japanese Tradition* (New York: Columbia University Press, 1965), 325–27.

Shinto? Why, by contrast, is Christianity a threat? What does he offer to do and warn he will do, in return? What does he see as the proper role of political authorities on religious issues?

Reading your message from afar, I can appreciate the immense expanse of water which separates us. As you have noted in your letter, my country, which is comprised of sixty-odd provinces, has known for many years more days of disorder than days of peace; rowdies have been given to fomenting intrigue, and bands of warriors have formed cliques to defy the court's orders. Ever since my youth, I have been constantly concerned over this deplorable situation. I studied the art of self-cultivation and the secret of governing the country. Through profound planning and forethought, and according to the three principles of benevolence, wisdom, and courage, I cared for the warriors on the one hand and looked after the common people on the other; while administering justice, I was able to establish security. Thus, before many years had passed, the unity of the nation was set on a firm foundation, and now foreign nations, far and near, without exception, bring tribute to us. Everyone, everywhere, seeks to obey my orders. . . . Though our own country is now safe and secure, I nevertheless entertain hopes of ruling the great Ming nation. I can reach the Middle Kingdom aboard my palace-ship within a short time. It will be as easy as pointing to the palm of my hand. I shall then use the occasion to visit your country regardless of the distance or the differences between us.

Ours is the land of the Gods, and God is mind. Everything in nature comes into existence because of mind. Without God there can be no spirituality. Without God there can be no way. God rules in times of prosperity as in times of decline. God is positive and negative and unfathomable. Thus, God is the root and source of all existence. This God is spoken of by Buddhism in India, Confucianism in China, and Shinto in Japan. To know Shinto is to know Buddhism as well as Confucianism.

As long as man lives in this world, Humanity will be a basic principle. Were it not for Humanity and Righteousness, the sovereign would not be a sovereign, nor a minister of state a minister. It is through the practice of Humanity and Righteousness that the foundations of our relationships between sovereign and minister, parent and child, and husband and wife are established. If you are interested in the profound philosophy of God and Buddha, request an explanation and it will be given to you. In your land one doctrine is taught to the exclusion of others, and you are not yet informed of the [Confucian] philosophy of Humanity and Righteousness. Thus there is no respect for God and Buddha and no distinction between sovereign and ministers. Through heresies you intend to destroy the righteous law. Hereafter, do not expound, in ignorance of right and wrong, unreasonable and wanton doctrines. A few years ago the so-called Fathers came to my country seeking to bewitch our men and women, both of the laity and clergy. At that time punishment was administered to them, and it will be repeated if they should return to our domain to propagate their faith. It will not matter what sect or denomination they represent— they shall be destroyed. It will then be too late to repent. If you entertain any desire of establishing amity with this land, the seas have been rid of the pirate menace, and merchants are permitted to come and go. Remember this.

As for the products of the south-land, acknowledgment of their receipt is here made, as itemized. The catalogue of gifts which we tender is presented on a separate paper. The rest will be explained orally by my envoy.

Postscript

Although it may seem as if this book covers every corner of the globe, it could have included still more material and been even thicker, for there were other significant religious transformations in this era: Islam continued to spread in East Africa and Southeast Asia, and pilgrims often returned from their trip to Mecca inspired to purify Islam in the same way that Muhammad al-Maghili was advocating in North Africa and the Songhay Empire. The rulers of the kingdom of Kongo in West Africa became Christian in the early sixteenth century and worked to convert their subjects. Many of the ideas of Christianity—a heavenly realm, priests with special powers, an initiation ritual involving water and signifying rebirth, angels and demons— were similar to religious ideas already present in West Africa, and the Christianity that emerged blended local elements as it did in Mesoamerica, or as Akbar's Divine Faith did in India.

In Bengal, the Hindu thinker who later took the name Krishna Caitanya (1486–1534) developed new spiritual insights and devotional practices to worship the great god Krishna; his most fervent followers believed that he became the goddess Radha and, like her, glowed golden in his longing for Krishna. They spread Caitanya's message of devotion to Krishna even to those who had not been born into Hindu families and eventually (through the Krishna Consciousness Society, the "Hare Krishnas") throughout the world in a pattern that had been earlier set by Christian missionaries and Muslim teachers.

In the 1570s in the mountains of Tibet, Sonam Gyatso, a Buddhist religious leader, or *lama*, declared that Altan Khan, the major Mongol lord of the time, was a reincarnation of Chinggis Khan, the greatest Mongol ruler of all time. Altan Khan in turn granted Sonam Gyatso the title "Cosmic Ocean lama," or Dalai Lama. Though the authority of the Dalai Lama was not accepted immediately, since then most Tibetan Buddhists have come to believe that he is successively reincarnated. The current Dalai Lama, Tenzin Gyatso (1935–), is the fourteenth in the succession (two of Sonam Gyatso's predecessors were posthumously declared to be the earliest incarnations), though it is difficult to say what will happen when he dies. Since the Chinese takeover of Tibet in 1959 the Dalai Lama has lived in exile and has asserted that he will not be reincarnated in territory ruled by China; in opposition to this, Chinese authorities claim the power to approve his successor.

The situation involving the Dalai Lama highlights the fact that religious transformations of the early modern period have powerful reverberations even today. This is certainly true with many of the developments discussed in this book. Conflicts between Protestants and Catholics resulted in violence in Northern Ireland throughout much of the twentieth century and as yet have not been completely resolved. Conflicts between Sunni and Shi'ite Muslims literally explode on the streets of Iraq nearly every day, and the treatment of non-Muslims living in Muslim lands continues to be an issue of debate. In 1984 the prime minister of India, Indira Gandhi, ordered an attack on the Sikh Golden Temple, during which hundreds of people were killed; in retaliation, Gandhi was assassinated by two of her bodyguards, who were Sikh, which led to violent anti-Sikh riots in which thousands died. Relations between Sikhs and Hindus continue to be tense in certain parts of India today. In the 1990s, a Muslim mosque in the Indian city of Ayodhya was torn down to make way for a Hindu temple at the urging of Hindu fundamentalists; in 2005 Muslim militants attacked the makeshift temple and were killed by security forces.

Along with conflict and violence, the creative blending of religious traditions that was so evident in the early modern period also continues. One of the most important—and most controversial—examples of such cultural synthesis is the Virgin of Guadalupe, who can serve as a fitting end to this book. In the seventeenth century, published texts in Spanish and Nahuatl told of the appearance of the Virgin Mary in 1531 to Juan Diego Cuauhtlatoatzin, an indigenous farmer and Christian convert, on a hill near Tenochtitlán (now within Mexico City). Speaking in Nahuatl, the apparition told Juan Diego that a church should be built at this site. Shortly afterward a church dedicated to the Virgin of Guadalupe was built and named after a monastery in Spain where various miracles associated with the Virgin Mary had been reported, including some involving Christian defeats of Muslim forces. The Mexican Virgin of Guadalupe soon far outstripped her Spanish counterpart in significance; preachers and teachers interpreted the Virgin's appearance as a sign of her special protection of indigenous people and *mestizos*, and pilgrims from all over Mexico began to make the trek to her shrine. The Virgin of Guadalupe was made patron of New Spain in 1746, and her banner was carried by soldiers in the Mexican War of Independence in 1810 and in the Mexican Revolution of 1910.

In the twentieth century, however, many scholars, including some members of the Mexican clergy, came to doubt whether the apparition had ever happened or if Juan Diego himself had even existed. They pointed out that written accounts were not published until over a century later and that church officials and missionaries active in central Mexico in 1531, such as those included in this book, made no mention of the event or of Juan Diego. Specialists in Nahuatl culture note that the hill where the apparition was reported was originally the site of a shrine to Coatlicue, the mother of Huitzilopochtli, and that aspects of the veneration of the Virgin of Guadalupe were also part of honoring Coatlicue or other Mexica mother goddesses; in their view, the colonial Catholic Church had simply invented the story as part of its efforts to strip Mexica holy sites of their original meaning. The Catholic Church has addressed these doubts resoundingly, declaring Guadalupe the patron of the whole American hemisphere in 1999 and raising Juan Diego to a saint in 2002; he is the first fully indigenous American to be canonized. (Rose of Lima [1586–1617] was the first American to be made a saint, but her ancestry was fully or largely Spanish.)

Many Mexicans have interpreted this canonization, like the Virgin of Guadalupe herself, as a symbol of the place of their heritage within the Catholic Church, while others view Juan Diego and Guadalupe as symbols of the destruction of indigenous culture. Intense controversies have emerged in recent years over the ways various artists have portrayed Guadalupe in their work, including the Chicana artist Alma Lopez's depiction of her dressed only in strands of roses. Lopez and other artists have justified their work by noting that through the centuries people have interpreted Guadalupe in whatever way they thought most empowering. Guadalupe, they argue, began as a symbol with multiple meanings, and they are simply continuing the tradition of synthesis that started with the first conversions in New Spain, a pattern you have no doubt found in many other traditions detailed in the documents here.

A Chronology of Early Modern Religious Transformations (1420s–1620s)

1420s Tlacaélel first gains power in the Mexica Empire.

1492 Ferdinand and Isabella conquer Granada; they also order the Jews to leave Spain or convert.

1493 Askia the Great gains throne in the West African Songhay Empire.

1490s Jews banished from North African oasis cities and prohibited from entering Songhay Empire.

1501 Ismail proclaims himself Shah of Iran.

1511 Erasmus writes *The Praise of Folly.*

1517 Ottoman Sultan Selim I conquers the Mamluk Empire.

1520 Martin Luther writes *The Freedom of a Christian.*

1520s Ignatius Loyola writes the *Spiritual Exercises.*
Cortés and his allies conquer the Mexica Empire.

1521 Guru Nanak establishes first Sikh community at Kartarpur.

1524 First Christian missionaries arrive in Mexico.

1526 Babur establishes the Mughal Empire.

1527 Wang Yangming writes "Questions on the *Great Learning.*"

1530s Safed in Palestine becomes a center of Kabbalistic thought.

1536 John Calvin first publishes the *Institutes of the Christian Religion.*

1537 Süleyman orders Sunni mosques built in every village of the Ottoman Empire.

1540 Bernardino de Sahagún writes a collection of sermons in Nahuatl.

1540 Society of Jesus (Jesuits) gains papal approval.

1545–1563 Council of Trent meets to make reforms and affirm Catholic doctrine.

1549 Francis Xavier first preaches Christianity in Japan.

1550s Al-Sharani composes his major writings.

1560s Teresa of Avila begins reforming Carmelite convents and writes *The Way of Perfection.*

Moses Cordovero writes *The Palm Tree of Deborah.*

1570s Guru Ram Das founds the city of Amritsar as a Sikh center.

1582 Akbar establishes the Divine Faith.

1587 Hideyoshi orders Jesuits to leave Japan.

1590 Abu'l Fazl composes the *Akbarnama.*

Li Zhi writes *A Book to Burn.*

1604 Guru Arjan Dev compiles the *Adi Granth.*

1614 Christians in Japan ordered to leave or convert.

1620 Hayashi Razan writes *Ruling and Living.*

1622 Ignatius Loyola and Teresa of Avila are canonized as saints.

Questions for Consideration

Note: Please see the chapter introductions for additional questions that focus on the documents in that chapter. The following questions suggest some of the ways in which the documents from several chapters offer examples of parallel, interwoven, or contrasting transformations. Many of the questions ask you to make comparisons, which is an important method for approaching historical topics, particularly in world history. When you make comparisons, be sure to consider similarities as well as differences and to think about possible reasons for the patterns that you find. Making historical comparisons does not just mean presenting first one case and then another, but identifying and analyzing similarities and differences.

INTERACTIONS

1. Many of the authors of the documents you have read showed hostility toward those of other faiths, and perhaps even more so toward those who had a different understanding of the same faith. Compare the writings of Teresa of Avila (Document 15), Muhammad al-Maghili (Document 19), Sultan Selim I and Shah Ismail (Document 20), and Toyotomi Hideyoshi (Document 41) on this issue.

2. The documents noted in question 1, and also the woodcut by Matthias Gerung (Document 13) and the writings of Desiderius Erasmus (Document 10), Katib Chelebi (Document 23), 'Abd ul-Qadir Bada'uni (Document 28), Li Zhi (Document 36), and Hayashi Razan (Document 39) depict enemies and those with differing viewpoints with very harsh verbal and visual images. Compare the portrayal of opponents in these documents.

3. Hostility toward those of other faiths led to war and persecution, which contributed to increased migration. One dramatic example was the expulsion of the Jews from Spain and the oasis cities of northern Africa. How might this have played a role in the development of

Lurianic Kabbalah? What other examples do you see in the documents of the impact of religiously motivated migrations?

4. Religious interactions sometimes occurred within an atmosphere of toleration, of which the best-known example was the court of Akbar (Documents 27–30). What other examples of toleration of religious differences do you find in the documents? Other than the support of a ruler such as Akbar, what conditions served to enhance toleration?

5. Akbar's Divine Faith (Document 30) is the clearest example from this era of religious synthesis, or the blending of different religious traditions. What other examples do you see in the documents? What examples do you see of those who opposed such blending? What reasons do the supporters and opponents of synthesis provide for their opinions?

6. Christianity and Islam were both actively seeking converts in new areas in this period. How would you compare the attitude of Bernardino de Sahagún (Documents 6 and 7), al-Maghili (Document 19), and Hosokawa Tama Gracia (Document 40) toward the process of conversion? What marked an individual as one who had truly undergone a religious conversion?

THE ROLE OF RELIGIOUS AND POLITICAL AUTHORITIES

7. The importance of an official hierarchy was debated within many traditions; some regarded this as essential, while others downplayed its importance. Compare the ideas of Erasmus (Document 10), Ignatius Loyola (Document 14), Pope Pius IV (Document 16), Wang Yangming (Documents 34 and 35), and Li Zhi (Document 36) on this issue.

8. Some writers asserted that close relations with the divine could be achieved by anyone, while others stressed that only long training or unusual insight could make one number among the spiritual elite. Compare the ideas of Loyola (Document 14), Abdulwahhab al-Sharani (Document 22), Isaac Luria (Document 25), and Li Zhi (Documents 36 and 37) on this issue.

9. Secular rulers were viewed as legitimate agents of religious change or the enforcement of doctrine in several documents. Compare the role in matters of religion given to secular rulers by Chimalpahin (Document 5), Loyola (Document 14), al-Sharani (Document 22), and Hayashi Razan (Document 39). How does this compare with Li Zhi's ideas (Document 36) on this issue?

10. Rulers themselves also weighed in on this issue. How do Sultan Selim and Shah Ismail (Document 20) and Hideyoshi (Document 41) view their authority in matters of religion?

UNDERSTANDINGS OF DIVINE AND HUMAN NATURE

11. Divine power is a common theme in many of the sources. What similarities and differences do you see in the ways divine power is portrayed in the Mexica materials (Documents 1–3), Olmos's *Final Judgment* (Document 8), Calvin's *Institutes* (Document 17), Sultan Selim's letter to Shah Ismail (Document 20), the *Guru Granth* (Document 31), and Hosokawa Tama Gracia's letter (Document 40)? What other qualities do these sources ascribe to God?

12. Some of the authors emphasize the transcendence of divine power and the distance between God or the gods and humans, while others emphasize proximity and connections. Compare the Mexica hymns (Documents 2 and 3), the writings of Teresa of Avila (Document 15), John Calvin (Document 17), Moses Cordovero (Document 24), and Guru Nanak (Document 31) on this issue.

13. Many of the authors use metaphors of darkness and light to describe the transition from unbelief to belief. How does this appear in the writings of Sahagún (Documents 6 and 7), Olmos (Document 8), Luria (Document 25), Abu'l Fazl (Document 27), and the Sikh wedding texts (Document 33)? Why might these be such common metaphors in religious texts? What other metaphors and symbols do authors use in their portrayals of the divine or of religious devotion?

14. Tlacaélel (Documents 3 and 4), Loyola (Document 14), and Teresa of Avila (Document 15) all describe religious devotion in military terms. What similarities and differences do you see in their words?

15. Compare ideas about human nature in the writings of Calvin (Document 17), Moses Cordovero (Document 24), Abu'l Fazl (Document 27), Guru Nanak (Document 31), and Wang Yangming (Document 34). Do these sources see goodness and evil as coming from inside or outside? What role does reason assume in guiding human nature according to these authors?

16. Compare ideas about the power of the human will in Loyola (Document 14), Calvin (Document 17), the words attributed to Akbar (Document 30), and Wang Yangming (Document 34). What effects does education have on human will and moral conduct for these authors?

MORAL BEHAVIOR AND THE OBLIGATIONS OF THE BELIEVER

17. Religious texts often set out the duties of a believer to God or the gods; how would you compare these as described in the Mexica hymns (Documents 2–4), Olmos's play (Document 8), and the writings of Luther (Documents 11 and 12), Loyola (Document 14), Teresa of Avila (Document 15), Cordovero (Document 24), Abraham Galante (Document 26), and Guru Nanak (Document 31)?

18. Loyola (Document 14), Calvin (Document 18), Galante (Document 26), Wang Yangming (Document 35), and Hayashi Razan (Document 39) provide specific rules for daily activities. Compare these rules. What seems to be the ultimate goal of these activities?

19. Many of the authors stress the importance of spiritual over earthly concerns. What similarities and differences do you see on this issue in the writings of Sahagún (Document 6), Olmos (Document 8), Teresa of Avila (Document 15), Guru Amar Das (Document 32), and Li Zhi (Document 37)?

20. Many of the authors comment on the value of good works and moral actions, though they take differing views. Compare the writings of Olmos (Document 8), Luther (Document 11), Loyola (Document 14), Calvin (Document 17), Cordovero (Document 24), the Sikh gurus (Documents 31 and 32), and Wang Yangming (Document 34) on this issue.

21. Many of the authors criticize certain religious practices as outward observances done without the proper inward belief or faith. Compare the opinions of Luther (Document 11), Katib Chelebi (Document 23), Guru Amar Das (Document 32), and Li Zhi (Document 36) on this issue.

22. The readings include several basic statements of faith developed in the sixteenth century, including those from Catholic Christianity (Document 16), Akbar's Divine Faith (Document 30), and Sikhism (Document 31). Compare these in terms of their idea of the nature of God and basic duties of the believer. For more comparisons, you may wish to investigate other sixteenth-century statements of faith, such as the Lutheran Augsburg Confession (www.ctsfw.edu/etext/boc/ac/) or the Calvinist Belgic Confession (www.canrc.org/resources/bop/belgic/).

23. Both Catholic (Documents 9 and 16) and Sufi (Documents 22 and 23) religious devotions involve the veneration of saints. What similarities and differences do you find in these documents?

24. Hymns, songs, and chants were an important means of expressing religious devotion. Compare the ways in which Mexica (Documents 2 and 3), Catholic (Document 7), and Sikh (Document 32) hymns or chants portray divine or holy figures.

25. Compare Chimalpahin's description of religious processions (Document 9) with Katib Chelebi's description of pilgrimages to tombs (Document 23). Both of these authors are educated observers. How might this have shaped their attitudes toward these devotional activities?

26. Religious thinkers had widely varying opinions about the relative value of marriage and celibacy. Compare the attitudes of Sahagún

(Document 7), Luther (Document 12), Loyola (Document 14), the Sikh gurus (Document 33), and Li Zhi (Document 37) on this issue.

27. In many of the sources, women have different spiritual obligations than men. Compare the spiritual duties of Mexica women (Document 4) with those set for women in Olmos's play (Document 8), Luther's wedding sermon (Document 12), Teresa of Avila's *The Way of Perfection* (Document 15), the Sikh wedding texts (Document 33), Li Zhi's letters (Document 37), and Hosokawa Tama Gracia's letter (Document 40).

28. Though many of the authors comment *about* women, the only two documents in this book *by* women are those of Teresa of Avila (Document 15) and Hosokawa Tama Gracia (Document 40). How would you compare their ideas about the role of women in religious transformations?

29. Many of the texts prescribe certain religious duties for men and set out ideals of masculine behavior. Compare those in the Mexica hymns (Documents 2 and 3), Sahagún's hymns (Document 7), Luther's sermon on marriage (Document 12), Loyola's *Spiritual Exercises* (Document 14), al-Sharani's description of a Sufi saint (Document 22), the Sikh wedding texts (Document 33), Li Zhi's letters (Document 37), and Hayashi Razan's text (Document 39).

30. The pictures of the Sufi brotherhood (Document 21), the scholars at Akbar's court (Document 29 and the cover), and the Chinese painter meditating (Document 38) all show men engaged in religious activities. How would you describe and compare these? What ideas about the relationship between gender and religion do these images suggest?

Selected Bibliography

MEXICAS

Carrasco, David. *City of Sacrifice: The Aztec Empire and the Role of Violence in Civilization*. Boston: Beacon, 2001. A sophisticated look at the role of religious violence in Mexica culture and in urban life since then.

———. *Religions of Mesoamerica: Cosmovision and Ceremonial Tradition*. Long Grove, Ill.: Waveland, 1989. A brief overview of religious structures, myths, and cosmology of Mesoamerica, especially the Maya and the Mexica, and also the continuity of indigenous traditions in postconquest Mexico.

Clendinnen, Inga. *Mexicas: An Interpretation*. Cambridge: Cambridge University Press, 1991. Explores the ways in which both leaders and ordinary Mexicas understood their world.

León-Portilla, Miguel. *Mexica Thought and Culture: A Study of the Ancient Nahuatl Mind*. Translated from the Spanish by Jack Emory Davis. Norman: University of Oklahoma Press, 1963. Discusses Nahuatl concepts of the universe, metaphysical and theological ideas, and notions of human nature and purpose.

———. *Pre-Columbian Literatures of Mexico*. Translated from the Spanish by Grace Lobanov and the author. Norman: University of Oklahoma Press, 1969. Analyzes various types of Nahuatl texts, including myths, sacred hymns, poetry, religious drama, chronicles, and histories.

CHRISTIANITY IN MEXICO

Burkhart, Louise M. *The Slippery Earth: Nahua-Christian Moral Dialogue in Sixteenth-Century Mexico*. Tucson: University of Arizona Press, 1989. Explores ways in which Nahuatl ideas about the structure of the cosmos, purity and pollution, health, and moral behavior shaped Christian understandings in Mexico.

Clendinnen, Inga. "Franciscan Missionaries in Sixteenth-Century Mexico," in *Disciplines of Faith: Religion, Patriarchy and Politics*, ed. James Obelkevich, Lyndal Roper, and Raphael Samuel. London: Routledge and Kegan Paul, 1987.

León-Portilla, Miguel. *Bernardino de Sahagún: First Anthropologist*. Translated by Mauricio J. Mixco. Norman: University of Oklahoma Press, 2002. Sympathetic biography of Sahagún, with extensive discussion of his interviews with indigenous elders.

Lockhart, James. *The Nahuas after the Conquest: A Social and Cultural History of the Indians of Central Mexico, Sixteenth through Eighteenth Centuries*. Stanford, Calif.: Stanford University Press, 1992. A massive analysis of all aspects of postconquest Nahua culture.

THE PROTESTANT AND CATHOLIC REFORMATIONS

Bireley, Robert. *The Refashioning of Catholicism: A Reassessment of the Counter Reformation*. Washington, D.C.: Catholic University Press of America, 1999. Presents a rethinking of the impact of the Catholic Reformation.

Bossy, John. *Christianity in the West, 1400–1700*. Oxford: Oxford University Press, 1985. A lively, brief overview of the major changes and continuities in this era.

Hsia, R. Po-chia. *A Companion to the Reformation World*. Oxford: Blackwell, 2004. Includes essays on a range of topics, each with a long bibliography.

———. *The World of Catholic Renewal, 1540–1770*. Cambridge: Cambridge University Press, 1998. Includes extended coverage of colonial Catholicism.

Lindbergh, Carter. *The European Reformations*. Oxford: Blackwell, 1996. A solid survey that focuses primarily on Protestants.

Mullett, Michael A. *The Catholic Reformation*. London: Routledge, 1999. A brief introduction.

Oberman, Heiko. *Luther: Man between God and the Devil*. New Haven, Conn.: Yale University Press, 1989. Provides a thorough grounding in Luther's thought.

O'Malley, John W., S.J. *The First Jesuits*. Cambridge, Mass.: Harvard University Press, 1993. Looks at the beginnings of the Jesuit order.

Weber, Alison. *Teresa of Avila and the Rhetoric of Femininity*. Princeton, N.J.: Princeton University Press, 1990. Explores Teresa's thought and use of language.

THE STATE AND THE INDIVIDUAL IN ISLAM

Burckhardt, Titus. *Introduction to Sufi Doctrine*. Bloomington, Ind.: World Wisdom, 2008. Presents a brief survey of Sufi teachings and methods.

Hoffman, Valerie J. *Sufism, Mystics, and Saints in Modern Egypt*. Columbia: University of South Carolina Press, 1995. Looks at Sufi spirituality in its historical context and includes material from many centuries.

Hunwick, John O. "Religion and State in the Songhay Empire, 1464–1591," in *Islam in Tropical Africa*, ed. I. M. Lewis. Oxford: Oxford University Press, 1966, 296–315.

———. *Jews of a Saharan Oasis: Elimination of the Tamantit Community.* New York: Marcus Weiner, 2006. Examines the effects of al-Maghili's preaching against Jews in North Africa and the Songhay Empire.

Savory, Roger. *Iran under the Safavids.* Cambridge: Cambridge University Press, 1980. A solid general survey that includes excellent coverage of religious and cultural developments.

Winter, Michael. *Egyptian Society under Ottoman Rule, 1517–1798.* London: Routledge, 1992. Traces social and religious developments.

———. *Society and Religion in Early Ottoman Egypt: Studies in the Writings of 'Abd al-Wahhab al-Sha'rani.* New Bruswick, N.J.: Transaction Books, 1982. Sets the thought of al-Sharani in its social, educational, and religious context and includes discussion of the Sufi orders.

MYSTICISM AND THE KABALLAH IN JUDAISM

Fine, Lawrence, ed. *Judaism in Practice from the Middle Ages through the Early Modern Period.* Princeton Readings in Religion. Princeton, N.J.: Princeton University Press, 2001. Collection of nearly forty translations of original texts, with extensive introductions by historians and scholars of Judaism.

———. *Physician of the Soul, Healer of the Cosmos: Isaac Luria and His Kabbalistic Fellowship.* Stanford, Calif.: Stanford University Press, 2003. Provides a thorough overview of the ideas and history of Lurianic Kabbalah.

RELIGIOUS BLENDING AT THE MUGHAL COURT

de Bary, Wm. Theodore, et al., eds. *Sources of Indian Tradition.* New York: Columbia University Press, 1958. Includes sources from many religious traditions, with extensive introductory commentary.

Habib, Irfan. *Akbar and His India.* Delhi: Oxford India, 2000. Collection of articles on the politics and culture of Akbar's India, edited by a major scholar of Indian history.

Richards, John F. *The Mughal Empire.* The New Cambridge History of India. Cambridge: Cambridge University Press, 1996. Narrative history of the Mughal Empire from 1526 to 1720.

SIKHISM

Cole, W. Owen. *Sikhism and Its Indian Context, 1469–1708: The Attitude of Guru Nanak and Early Sikhism to Indian Religious Beliefs and Practices.* London: Darton, Longman & Todd, 1984. Explores the relationship between Sikhism and other religions of India.

Grewal, J. S. *The Sikhs of the Punjab*. New Cambridge History of India. Cambridge: Cambridge University Press, 1991. Examines the life and beliefs of Guru Nanak and his successors and sets Sikhism within the context of the Mughal Empire and subsequent governments.

McLeod, W. H. *Guru Nanak and the Sikh Religion*. Oxford: Clarendon Press, 1968. Study of the life and teachings of Guru Nanak.

———. *Sikhism*. London: Penguin, 1997. A brief, general introduction to Sikhism.

Singh, Khuswant. *The Illustrated History of the Sikhs*. New York: Oxford University Press, 2006. Traces the Sikh faith from its founding to today.

CONFUCIANISM AND OTHER TRADITIONS IN CHINA

Chang, Chün-mai. *The Development of Neo-Confucian Thought*. London: Vision, 1958. A brief survey of Confucianism from the Song through the Qing dynasties.

de Bary, Wm. Theodore. *Neo-Confucian Orthodoxy and the Learning of the Mind-and-Heart*. New York: Columbia University Press, 1981. Traces Confucian thought about the relationship of learning and action in China and Japan.

Taylor, Rodney. *The Religious Dimensions of Confucianism*. Albany: State University of New York Press, 1990. Overview of Confucianism as a religious tradition.

Thompson, Laurence G. *Chinese Religion: An Introduction*. Belmont, Calif.: Wadsworth Publishing, 1995. Discusses Buddhism, Daoism, Confucianism, and folk religion as aspects of Chinese culture.

Tu, Wei-ming. *Neo-Confucian Thought in Action: Wang Yang-ming's Youth (1472–1509)*. Berkeley: University of California Press, 1976. Provides an intensive analysis of the forces that shaped Wang Yangming.

RELIGIOUS TRADITIONS IN JAPAN

Boxer, C. R. *The Christian Century in Japan, 1549–1650*, rev. ed. Berkeley: University of California Press, 1967. A classic study of Catholicism in early modern Japan.

Earhart, H. Byron. *Japanese Religion: Unity and Diversity* and *Religion in the Japanese Experience: Sources and Interpretations*. Belmont, Calif.: Wadsworth Publishing, 2004 and 1997. Provide excellent overviews.

Ellison, George. *Deus Destroyed: The Image of Christianity in Early Modern Japan*. Cambridge, Mass.: Harvard University Press, 1973. Thoroughly analyzes opposition to Christianity in Japan.

Ward, Haruko Narata. *Women Religious Leaders in Japan's Christian Century, 1549–1650*. Burlington, Vt.: Ashgate, 2008. An insightful examination of the role of women as supporters and opponents of Christianity in Japan.

Acknowledgments (continued from p. iv)

Document 7: *Bernardino de Sahagun's Psalmodia Christiana* (Christian Psalmody), translated by Arthur J. O. Anderson (Salt Lake City: University of Utah Press, 1993).

Document 8: Andres de Olmos, "Final Judgment," in Barry D. Sell and Louise M. Burkhart, eds. *Nahuatl Theater, Volume 1: Death and Life in Colonial Nahua Mexico* (Norman: University of Oklahoma Press, 2004). Copyright © 2004 The University of Oklahoma Press. All Rights Reserved.

Document 10: Hoyt H. Hudson, translator, *Praise of Folly by Erasmus.* © 1941 Princeton University Press, 1969 renewed. Reprinted by permission of Princeton University Press.

Document 11: From *Luther's Works* Volume 31 by Martin Luther, edited by Harold J. Grimm and Helmut T. Lehmann. Copyright 1957 Fortress Press. Reproduced by special permission of Augsburg Fortress Publishers.

Document 14: Excerpt from *The Spiritual Exercises of St. Ignatius of Loyola* by Louis J. Puhl, S.J. (Newman Press, 1951). Reprinted with permission of Loyola Press. To order copies of this book call 800-621-1008 or go to www.loyolapress.com.

Document 15: Selections from Teresa of Avila, *The Way of Perfection*, translated and edited by E. Allison Peters (New York: Image Books, 1964), pp. 20–22, 25, 27.

Document 16: "Tridentine Profession of Faith," in Henry Bettenson, ed., *Documents of the Christian Church* (Oxford: Oxford University Press, 1963.) Reproduced by permission of Oxford University Press.

Document 19: © The British Academy 1985. Reproduced by permission from *Sharia in Songhay: The Replies of al-Maghili to the Questions of Askia al-Hajj Muhammad*, edited and translated by John O. Hunwick.

Document 20: "Letters from Selim and Ismael," translated by John F. Woods in William H. McNeill and Marilyn Robinson Waldman, eds., *The Islamic World* (Oxford: Oxford University Press, 1973). Reproduced by permission of Oxford University Press.

Document 23: Katib Chelebi, *The Balance of Truth*, translated by G. L. Lewis (London: George Allen and Unwin, 1957).

Documents 24 and 25: Pages 83–85, 88, 149 from *The Essential Kabbalah* by Daniel C. Matt. Copyright © 1995 by Daniel C. Matt. Reprinted by permission of HarperCollins Publishers.

Document 26: Excerpts from *Safed Spirituality: Rules of Mystical Piety, the Beginning of Wisdom,* translated by/edited by Lawrence Fine, copyright © 1984 by Lawrence Fine. Paulist Press, Inc., New York/Mahwah, NJ. Reprinted by permission of Paulist Press, Inc. www.paulistpress.com.

Documents 28 and 30: 'Abd ul-Qadir Bada'uni, *"Selected Histories"* and Muhsi-i-Fani, "School of Religion" in Wm. Theodore de Bary, et al., eds., *Sources of Indian Tradition* (New York: Columbia University Press, 1958).

Documents 31 and 32: *Selections from the Sacred Writings of the Sikhs*, translated by Dr. Trilochan Singh, et al. (New York: Macmillan, 1960).

Document 33: W. H. McLeod, Emeritus Professor of History, University of Otago, Dunedin, New Zealand.

Documents 34 and 35: Wang Yangming, "Questions on the *Great Learning*" and "The Community Compact for Southern Ganzhou" in Wm. Theodore de Bary and Irene Bloom, comp., *Sources of Chinese Tradition,* 2nd Ed. (New York: Columbia University Press, 1999).

Document 36: Li Zhi, "A Book to Burn (Fenshu)" in Wm. Theodore de Bary and Irene Bloom, comp., *Sources of Chinese Tradition*, 2nd Ed. (New York: Columbia University Press, 1999).

Document 37: Reprinted with the permission of The Free Press, a Division of Simon & Schuster Adult Publishing Group, from *Chinese Civiliation: A Sourcebook*, 2nd Ed. by Patricia Buckley Ebrey. Copyright © 1993 by Patricia Buckley Ebrey. All rights reserved.

Document 39: David Lu, *Japan: A Documentary History* (Armonk, NY: M. E. Sharpe, 1997), pp. 245–47.

Document 41: Toyotomi Hideyoshi, "Letter to the Viceroy of the Indies," in Ryusaku Tsunoda, Wm. Theodore de Bary, and Donald Keene, eds., *Sources of Japanese Tradition* (New York: Columbia University Press, 1965).

Index

175